The Definitive
GUIDE TO
FOOTBALL
PROGRAMMES

The Definitive
GUIDE TO
FOOTBALL
PROGRAMMES

Julian Earwaker

An illustrated guide to the hobby
of football programme collecting

CHAPTER 6 PUBLISHING · IPSWICH

© 1987
Chapter 6 Publishing
Turret Lane, Ipswich, Suffolk, IP4 1DL

Designed, edited and published by Chapter 6
Cover design and colour photography by A. J. Spicer

ISBN 1 870 70700 1

Printed in Great Britain by
Richard Clay Ltd, Bungay, Suffolk

Acknowledgements

Grateful acknowledgements to: The Programme Association for Collectors and Traders (PACT) for permission to reproduce 'PACT Guidelines for Postal Offers' and to Dick Rattray (Secretary) for his comments and advice; David Stacey, Ray Spiller, John Litster, for their relevant material and articles; and to David Kirkby, who kindly gave permission to use his material as a basis for 'The Hobby Abroad'. Thanks also to Andrew Spicer, for artwork and design; Bernard Jasper, for his excellent command of the English language; Susan Watkins, for her meticulous attention to detail; John Eastwood, who provided the introduction to this book and who also advised and encouraged; and to my family, for their continued support, especially Richard, without whom this book would not have been produced.

Contents

1
Introduction

'Programme! Programme!'

by John Eastwood
Author of *The Men who Made the Town*
and *Canary Citizens*

As one approaches any British football ground the familiar cry of the programme seller is sure to greet you and long queues of spectators form in front of the programme huts and stands in order to secure their particular souvenir of the forthcoming match. While you are of course all familiar with present-day programmes our purpose here is to look back into the distant past and study the offerings of yesteryear. We chart the progress from the days when a programme was little more than a single team sheet simply informing the public of the combatants on view to the present-day situation where most clubs issue a glossy magazine containing news and views of a much more general nature.

The Football Association was formed after a meeting that took place at the Freemason's Tavern, Lincoln's Inn Fields, London, on Monday 26 October 1863. The idea behind this historic meeting was to adopt a standard set of rules, and to generally promote the game of football throughout the length and breadth of the land. As all the delegates present came from the South of England, indeed nearly all represented clubs in the London area, many years were to pass before it could be stated that Association Football was a truly national game.

Almost a decade passed before the FA Cup, or the Football Association Challenge Cup competition to give it its full title, was first suggested to the Football Association committee by C. W. Alcock, the secretary. The first FA Cup final was played on Saturday 16 March 1872 at the Kennington Oval (now of course more noted for cricketing activities) between Wanderers and the Royal Engineers. The suggestion that the Football Association should promote competitive matches, put forward

11

as we have seen by its own secretary Charles Alcock, proved extremely valuable in helping to popularise the game across the country – and Alcock didn't do so badly himself – he was the captain of the winning Wanderers team.

Although the majority of the fifteen entrants for this first FA Cup competition came from the Home Counties there were two notable exceptions: Donington School from Lincolnshire and the Queen's Park club from Glasgow. On account of the huge travelling distances involved Queen's Park were exempted until the semi-final stage. When they finally joined the competition and met the Wanderers in London on Monday 4 March 1872 the result was a 0–0 draw, but owing to lack of funds a replay never took place and Wanderers, rather fortuitously, were left to take their place in the first FA Cup final. The exercise, however, proved to be fruitful, competitive football was firmly established, and during the next season the first international between England and Scotland was played at Hamilton Crescent, Glasgow, on Saturday 30 November 1872.

Now we come to the burning issue of whether or not programmes were ever issued for any of the above-mentioned games. Certainly the matches were widely publicised in the press of the day and two thousand people attended the first FA Cup final and about four thousand turned up for the first Scotland v. England match. It also appears very likely that in addition to the newspaper inserts, bills or posters would have been printed and exhibited in prominent places, but as to the issuing of a team sheet or programme – who knows – none are known to survive.

It is certain, however, that the earliest offerings were mere team sheets, and Phil Shaw, writing in his excellent book on programme collecting (*Collecting Football Programmes* – Granada Publishing Limited 1980), puts forward a team sheet from a friendly between those great old rivals Queen's Park, Glasgow, and Wanderers as possibly the oldest existing programme. The match took place on Saturday 9 October 1875 in Glasgow and interestingly the players were identified by the colour of their caps or stockings, rather like the modern jockey. It must have been a colourful sight, for the Queen's Park centre front (forward) wore red stockings and Charles Alcock, his opposite number, was distinguished by a blue and white chequered cap. Furthermore the crowd was requested in bold lettering at the base of the sheet not to push forward and 'strain the ropes'.

On Saturday 1 November 1884 Notts Association met London Association in a representative friendly at Trent Bridge, Nottingham, and an eight-page programme was produced by the local printers George Richards of Greyhound Street, Nottingham. The full teams were given on the front cover, Notts Association played in a 2–3–5 formation while London preferred to utilise two backs, two half-backs and six forwards. Apart from the usual advertisements for sports outfitters and tobacconists the rest of the offering contained much useful information such as the draw for the first round of the FA Cup, the Notts fixtures for 1884/85, the results of the 1883/84 matches and the Nottingham Forest results and fixtures. It is interesting to note that no less than five Nottingham clubs took part in the first round of the FA Cup that year: Nottingham Forest, Notts County, Nottingham Olympic, Nottingham Wanderers and Nottingham Rangers. It has not been established if this was indeed the first 'proper' programme, and it probably never will, for new material is always being unearthed, but it is certainly a fine example of a very early offering.

The Nottingham printers George Richards certainly went out of their way to develop this side of their business, they already produced books and pamphlets on Nottingham cricket, and their name crops up again on a team sheet produced for the 1886/87 Suffolk Association Cup final. The match was played at Portman Road between Ipswich Association (forerunner of Ipswich Town FC) and Ipswich School on Saturday 12 March 1887. There are many other examples of their work still in existence – perhaps they produced a team sheet or programme for an early match in which YOUR club took part!

We now move on to the latter part of the 1880's and the

arrival of professionalism. William McGregor, a Scottish draper living in Birmingham, an official of Aston Villa FC and spokesman for the Birmingham FA, proposed that the leading clubs of the day should meet and discuss the possibility of forming a football league. On Friday 23 March 1888, the eve of the FA Cup final, representatives of the leading clubs met at Anderton's Hotel in London and their conference led directly to the formation of the Football League. The first Football League matches took place on Saturday 8 September 1888, and now that the idea of regular competitive professional football had been established club programmes gradually became an accepted part of the game.

Early programmes were still essentially team sheets containing little or no editorial content, but because of the innately commercial nature of Football League matches they encouraged a profusion of advertising. Over the years the magazines dealing with the hobby of programme collecting have reproduced many examples of late Victorian issues and from the 1897 FA Cup final offering we learn that a case of eight-year-old Scotch whisky would have cost a mere forty-two old shillings (£2.10). Also included is a rather snappy advertisement for a weekly sports paper —

> People swear by it
> Rivals swear at it
> Agents pant for it
> The public fight for it
> and YOU can buy it EVERYWHERE

Carter's finest grass seed, we are told, is used at Lord's, the Oval, Aston Villa and Crystal Palace, and Grant's Morella cherry brandy, we are reliably informed, is not only most comforting in chilly weather but is 'the best tonic going for football players'.

The first club to fully exploit the potential of the programme as an informative magazine was Aston Villa FC. The first issue of 'The Villa News and Record' appeared on Saturday 1 September 1906 when Villa entertained Blackburn Rovers in a

League match. The offering contained 18 pages of news, views, pictures and statistics and was later copied in some respects by other leading Football League clubs. A nice story with a programme flavour was told about Scott Duncan soon after he was appointed as the manager of Ipswich Town FC in 1937. Ipswich had recently turned professional but had not yet acquired Football League status. Asked by anxious supporters how he would achieve the treasured goal he replied thus – 'Yes, we must increase the playing strength, and yes, we must improve facilities at the ground, but first we must produce a club programme fit for a Football League team.' He soon produced the goods on the programme front and Town were quickly elected to the League.

Before we take a closer look at the programmes of the 1930's we must mention a few earlier offerings. In the years around the First World War several printers attempted, with varying degrees of success, to produce a National football programme. The Scottish version, published by the Exchange Printing Company of Glasgow, first appeared about 1907 and continued until well into the 1930's. It consisted of four pages measuring 10″ × 6″. The first page gave the complete day's fixtures and this was followed by the line-ups for the various Scottish engagements on that particular day. A half-time scoreboard appeared on page three while the back page was taken up by a League chart made up to include the previous week's results. In addition there was, of course, a liberal sprinkling of advertisements on all the pages.

Other companies printed and published programmes for various clubs on a franchise basis. One such organisation involved in this activity in the 1920's was L. & H. Blower Brothers of Bushey. In additon to producing the Watford programme they also extended their services to Huddersfield Town and Rotherham County. The offerings consisted of eight A5-size pages containing some editorial features but were mainly taken up with the usual advertising.

How would you like to own one of the most sought-after programmes in the history of football – and only pay a threepenny piece for the privilege? Well it could have been done, but first you would have had to have attended the celebrated first FA Cup final at Wembley in 1923. Imagine the thrill of approaching the magnificent new stadium to watch Bolton Wanderers take on West Ham United. It is said that about 150,000 people actually forced their way into the ground and many more were left to follow events from the surrounding area. A mere threepenny piece would have secured the resplendent 28-page commemorative programme containing features on the two teams and a reflection on the FA Cup competition to date. Copies in good condition are now quite rare but do still surface from time to time. It was a great thrill to recently discover that a man living in the same street as myself has kept a copy which is in near mint condition. He recalls vividly how as a young man he and two of his friends made their way up to Wembley by train on that late April afternoon all those years ago. He never claims to have seen the legendary policeman on the conspicuous white horse but he has kept his admission ticket and even his cheap-day rail return. His lasting memory of a very exciting day is encapsulated in his much treasured programme. As he jokingly adds – 'what a great pity I didn't get a few more copies'.

As we move into the 1930's it is noticeable that the general standard and pride in club programmes is seen to improve. Still present are the great wedges of advertising and, by modern standards, rather bald and rudimentary statistical matter but more exuberance is reflected in a much improved style and design. As an example we might well look to the silver jubilee celebrations of George V and his Queen in 1935. Many programme editors chose to regale their front covers with pictures of the couple and later, after the succession of King George VI, messages of congratulation appeared in many club offerings.

I have a copy of a late 1930's programme in front of me at present. The date is Saturday 27 August 1938 and Ipswich Town are entertaining Southend United in the old Third Division South – Town's first match in the Football League. The programme cost 2d. and measures some 8" × 10". The issue was printed by the *East Anglian Daily Times* and from a small figure on the base of the back cover we can deduce that the print run was 10,000. There are 24 pages in all, consisting of nine pages of advertising, seven pages of various messages and editorial, five pages devoted to the line-ups and visitors, a page of fixtures, and a page each on 'soccer pals' and feminine topics. In addition there is a handsome photographic reproduction of the players, officials and directors of the club which has been pasted between pages 2 and 3.

The 'soccer pals' feature is of course typically 1930's and the editor, who calls himself 'The Spectator', opens his account by wishing all 'soccer pals' from nine to ninety best wishes and good luck for the coming season. He promises to fill his weekly page with stories, jokes, cartoons and readers' letters and expresses his desire for readers to contribute as many as they can. His overall theme is adventure and the first article spotlights the newly opened Ipswich Airport. He goes on to describe the exhilaration of entering the new terminus and striding across the tarmac to the waiting plane. Once in the air he likens the fields below to 'so many handkerchiefs coloured by the yellows and browns of ripening crops, green meadows and the dark tilled land, the whole taking on a beautiful patchwork effect' – good stuff indeed. On the facing page we see that the ladies and girls (and many used to attend matches around this time) were not forgotten. They had their very own page of 'feminine topics' which included a report of a visit to a local department store and finishes off with a recipe for savoury pancakes – looking back now it may all appear rather tame and sexist but I am assured by an elderly couple living nearby that both features were eagerly anticipated and always thoroughly well received.

Another much prized feature of inter-war programmes was the beloved cartoon. Leading clubs such as Manchester United, Chelsea, West Ham United and Tottenham Hotspur were especially prominent in this field and their offerings were often extremely amusing and informative. Somehow the cartoonist's art and skill managed to convey a message that a four-colour picture has never accomplished. We were especially fortunate here at Ipswich for not only did Oliver Westlake always provide a poignant offering for the late 1930's programmes, he also supplied an after-match cartoon for the Saturday evening sports paper. I often thought that I learned more about a particular match and the characters that took part in them from studying the lampoon in the evening paper than by reading through a six-hundred-word match report. What a pity that we no longer have the opportunity of seeing them.

In the main the demise of the cartoon feature was brought about by improvements in printing technology and the ready availability of high-quality photography, but there were other factors at work – the Second World War and paper shortages. Organised football was totally disrupted by the war effort, young men were called to the flag and distinguished careers left to founder upon the rocks of time. Some competitive football was possible but it was a shadow of its former self. Programmes produced for wartime matches often reverted to a single team sheet and much of the good work achieved throughout the past decade was lost for ever.

When the war eventually came to an end soccer was left to pick up the pieces. Paper shortages, and in some cases outright rationing, continued throughout the boom years of the 1940's. The programmes produced at this time were scant, inadequate and printed on poor quality paper, often conveying little more than the bare essentials. It was a time of building, a time of replenishment, and despite the great escalation and rekindled interest in our national game there was little opportunity for commercial development. To demonstrate the interest in football during the late 1940's we put forward the following – no fewer than 143,570 spectators witnessed the Scottish FA Cup semi-final at Hampden Park between Rangers and Hibernian on Saturday 27 March 1948 and a Football League record crowd of 83,260 saw the clash between Manchester United and Arsenal on Saturday 17 January 1948. Technically speaking the last named match took place on a neutral ground as Old Trafford was being refurbished after extensive war damage and United played their home games at Maine Road, the home of course of Manchester City FC.

The 1950's saw little overall advance in the standard of club programmes. True, colour returned to the front covers and the quality of paper used steadily improved, but the design and layout features often remained static. Looking back at my own Ipswich Town collection recently I noticed that between the 1949/50 and 1957/58 seasons the cover design and layout hardly changed at all. When change was implemented at the start of the 1958/59 campaign it could hardly be said that it was a change for the better — along came the small square pocket-sized issues which retained the same façade for the whole of the season and annoyingly did not contain the date of the match or the name of the opponents on the cover. I noticed too that many of our opponents also employed rather monotonous and lifeless creations. Such was life in the 1950's — but in defence it must be noted that the price of programmes remained remarkably stable throughout the period — the Ipswich Town offerings of 1949/50 cost 3d. each and they still cost the same during the 1957/58 season!

The diminutive and impudent frame of 'World Cup Willie' probably did more to change the face of footballing merchandise than anyone else. He was the mascot and symbol of the 1966 World Cup competition staged here in England and by the end of that marvellous summer he proved himself to be much more than a passive motif — he was a super salesman. There were 'World Cup Willie' hats, badges, scarves and sweaters — he was as much of a star as Bobby Moore and his triumphant team. Football clubs were perhaps as surprised as anyone else that the public had exhibited a desire to purchase such lucrative paraphernalia and the message certainly did not go unheeded. The latter part of the decade saw an unprecedented increase and improvement in all forms of football commodities which naturally included the hitherto humble club programme. New methods of production were introduced, which led in turn to some mighty price increases, and it was around this time that many clubs made use of the national inserts supplied by the Football League.

Perhaps inspired by the greatly improved offerings the hobby of collecting football programmes really took off in the early 1970's. Perhaps too the 1970's proved to be years of consolidation after the vigorous social changes witnessed during the previous decade. Collecting as a hobby was certainly nothing new to mankind but the explosion that occurred in all fields of accumulation around this period was probably a logical reaction to the disposable nature of modern society. A collection of programmes provides a lasting link with the past and what can be more relaxing on a long winter evening than a ramble though the memories of our yesterdays?

I often wonder what my late grandfather would have said if he knew that huge sums of money were being exchanged for the programmes of his day. I'm sure he would have been surprised and probably slightly amused. I wonder also what he would have thought of today's prices – he would never have believed that some clubs charge £1.00 for a single issue!

2
The Programme

programme ('prəʊgræm) *n.* a written or printed list of the events, performers, etc., in a public performance.

The Programme

A football programme today is a multi-purpose publication, fulfilling different roles for collectors, supporters, and football clubs alike. It serves as a small but important part of a club's public image, as a souvenir of the match, a collector's item, and as reading material for pre-match, half-time and post-match entertainment. Programmes form, individually, a small part of the overall 'encyclopedia' of soccer facts and information that a collection represents.

The role of the programme has greatly increased in importance, with growing interest in football programmes and souvenirs in recent years. Improved printing and production methods, and a more professional approach by most editors, have combined to produce today's colourful, informative and glossy publications. The range of articles has increased from mere team line-ups in early programmes to the multitude of photographs, articles, features, and news items of the modern issue. Details of visiting teams, club fixtures, results, statistics, puzzles, competitions, articles by players, managers and directors, historical 'flashbacks', and match details, are all integral parts of today's programme. Colour photography has also greatly aided the visual appeal of the football programme. Somehow though, these programmes still lack the character, grace, and elegance, of some of the hobby's earlier offerings.

Each programme represents a fraction of football history; the rise and fall of famous clubs, and the careers of household names, are thus preserved in print for future reference. They also provide a fascinating insight into the society of past eras; old advertisements, cartoons, and the somewhat quaint, stilted, writing style of the period, holding particular fascination.

Programmes today also represent big business for football clubs, forming a vital source of income for many clubs involved in the daily struggle for survival, in a highly competitive environment, faced with increasingly fickle public support. This growth in commercial importance has been allied with a dramatic upsurge in prices, far outreaching inflation rates, and making a nonsense of technological innovation and the cheaper production methods now available to programme producers. With total attendances in the Football League currently reaching over 16 million each season, while nowhere near the peak of 40 million achieved during the 1940's, this represents seasonal programme sales of approximately 5 million copies. With most prices ranging from 50p to £1 for league programmes, the total revenue available to clubs is impressive.

The upsurge in prices has seriously affected the collecting market, however, with those collectors operating on restricted budgets finding their range of collectable items being limited still further. This is particularly disappointing for the young collector, and can act as a considerable disincentive to enter the hobby.

The definition of a football programme has always been a subject of great debate within the hobby. Recent seasons have seen a somewhat disturbing trend of press releases and directors' team sheets being masqueraded as programmes, for what would otherwise be matches without issues. Some programme 'producers' let their enthusiasm cloud their better judgement, and seem intent upon obtaining a programme for every match, even to the extent of hand-writing their own issues. While a few collectors applaud the initiative shown by some of their fellow enthusiasts, at the same time dismissing such issues as being merely interesting souvenirs, most agree that such publications are devalued if not produced by the host club. This leads many to include the term 'indigenous' in their definitions of a programme.

At the other extreme, are those collectors who disregard any item not completely complying with their carefully prepared, pre-set, definitions. Such definitions usually include date, time, venue, teams, officials and the words 'official programme' as prerequisite. Most also insist that the game must take place, and that the programme must be available for sale, at the ground, on the day of the match. Foreign issues, postponed matches, newspaper productions, free issues, and club magazines, all inevitably cause some confusion. Similarly, not all official programmes actually state 'official programme' on, or inside, the publication. Other problems have been caused by the issue of programmes for some 'closed door' matches, for example, the 1984/5 Burton Albion v. Leicester City FA Cup third round, enforced cup replay at Coventry, for which programmes were made available. Single sheet photocopied issues usually cause collectors a few headaches, with clubs reproducing on demand, and collectors and dealers frequently doing likewise.

Too much debate on this subject, whilst perhaps inevitable, is seemingly pointless, for at the end of the day, it must fall to the individual collector to decide whether a publication is acceptable or not, and whether money will be spent on pur-chasing that item.

Programme compilation and editing

Although technological advancements and improved printing techniques have greatly aided the programme producer, the ultimate success of a production lies in the hands of the programme editor. Too many programmes fit into a tired, standard format, of stereotyped articles and similar presentation. Today's editor is engaged in a constant battle to produce interesting, original, attractive, and informative issues.

One of the main features of the club programme is the focus upon local news and issues. National enclosures such as the 'Football League Review' of the late 1960's and early 1970's, and the Maybank Press's brief flirtation with national centre-page inserts in the early 1980's, have never really enjoyed much popularity with the programme-buying public. The main purchasers of the match day programme are the home supporters, and original and interesting reading material, with a pronounced local bias, usually ensures popularity with the native population.

Prospective programme editors could do worse than to study the progress of the FA Cup Final programme. No other fixture can match the selling potential of this match, and over 300,000 copies of the programme are sold each season. Recent changes in format have caused concern amongst some collectors, but there can be no denying that the large page format, light card cover, pages of excellent reading material, and glossy presentation, are both modern and original.

For most editors, the preparation and presentation of the programme is essentially a labour of love. Only the larger clubs can afford to pay for an editor, and for most, benefits in kind, brief recognition by the public, and the satisfaction of seeing a completed production, week after week, are the only rewards. Many clubs turn to enthusiasts amongst their own supporters, rather than relying upon the worn clichés of the local journalist, or placing the burden upon the already over-worked club secretary. The job requires dedication, enthusiasm, innovation, imagination, diplomacy (both in satire and in fact), organisational ability, and sheer hard work. Editorial discretion is frequently required, even when dealing with non-controversial subjects. Printing deadlines can cause considerable difficulties, especially during spells of prolonged bad weather, when it is uncertain whether a programme will be required or not, and continued postponements lead to rapidly dated material. During the Christmas period, articles often have to be written many days in advance of the actual match, in order to meet the printer's holiday deadlines. Besides the preparation of first team match programmes, most editors are also responsible for reserve and youth team issues. These are usually A4 photocopied single sheets, or folded to form four page, A5 issues. The editor's job involves long hours, seeking to provide the public with interesting and informative reading material. It is a hard task, and one that all collectors and programme purchasers would do well to appreciate.

The motivation for producing a football programme, in all cases, should be to entertain and inform the supporter at the match. Programmes produced merely for the benefit of collectors are of dubious value (and usually of dubious origin), but in many cases, the collector and the supporter are synonymous. Selecting a balance of features, articles, statistics and pictures can be a difficult task. One of the best ways of deciding upon content for a match programme, is to study the marking categories of annual programme awards.

In 1965, the British Programme Collectors Club originated national programme awards, judged upon six categories. These covered:

COST, looking for reasonable pricing and value for money.
COVER, looking for clear details, attractive design, and frequent cover changes.

CONTENT, with emphasis upon reading material.

INSERTS, which were not popular with judges.

SIZE, with very small, or, conversely, outsized, newspaper formats being unpopular.

VOUCHERS, preferably to be avoided at all costs, but, if used, definitely not to be printed on the cover.

Today, there are several different programme awards presented at the end of each season. Marking categories have been expanded to include paper and print quality, range of articles (considering such issues as club information, club officials' columns, visitors' coverage, reserve/youth details, historical features, club and player news, and national news), use of colour, photographs, comparative changes (between seasons), and advertising content. Attention is also given to the standard or content, the mixture of articles and features, aesthetic qualities, and, comparative to other club programmes, value.

Imitation may be the sincerest form of flattery, but editors should strive to avoid producing the dull, lifeless, stereotyped, programmes that seem to form the bulk of so many collections. They should also take care not to infringe upon the copyright of others. The continued reproduction of players' pen-pictures, without the knowledge or the consent of the originators, is a classical example of this, and a particular source of annoyance when reproduced without even the slightest acknowledgement.

Advertising content may be a source of irritation to the purists within the hobby of programme collecting, but it bears considerable commercial significance for the football club. Not all clubs will find themselves in the position that Gainsborough Town found themselves in during the 1985/6 season. This little club, then in the Dryborough Northern League, Division 2, produced a 100 page programme, thought to be the largest in Britain, for only 25p. Containing 92 pages of advertising content, and sponsorship totalling £3,500, this production was a tremendous achievement for a club operating with very limited resources. With any significant amount of advertising content, the match day programme can become self-financing, and sales subsequently represent almost pure profit for the club. Balanced against this, is the editor's task to present interesting and entertaining reading material, which pages of advertising content can hardly claim to represent.

Rarity and value

It is not the purpose of this publication to serve as a definitive price guide for the hobby of programme collecting. Prices are readily available from dealers' catalogues and the 'for sale' pages of publications within the hobby and, ultimately, the market laws of supply and demand will settle the price for individual items. Generally, buyers set their own price for rare programmes, with many individuals using advertisements, listing rare wanted items, with stated maximum prices that they are prepared to pay. This is the inverse of the dealer's offers list system, where rare items are listed, with stated minimums, and postal offers are invited from collectors.

Rarity of items frequently relates to age, although there are many examples of modern issues that are particularly obscure, or difficult to obtain.

Pre-World War One issues are rare indeed, although many fine examples of these programmes can be found in private collections around the country. Pre-World War Two programmes are also scarce, although there is little rationale behind the scarcity of individual pre-war English League club programmes. A general guide to scarcity can usually be discerned from the demands of collectors and their wants lists. Naturally, war has been responsible for the loss of a great many early programmes, with collections being abandoned, or destroyed, along with many other precious ephemera and belongings.

Owing to the enforced, stringent economical measures, wartime issues, and also many immediate post-war programmes, tended to be printed on poor quality, flimsy paper, and inevitably, many were destined to become lost or damaged. Through the 1940's and 1950's, programmes are still sought-after by many collectors, and a good number of these issues are now quite rare.

For programmes produced in the last 25 years or so, there are no hard and fast rules regarding value or rarity, most issues being sought-after for unique and diverse reasons. It is often futile, too, trying to predict which current programmes will be valuable in the years ahead.

Programmes of ex-league clubs, such as Accrington Stanley, Gateshead, Third Lanark, and, more recently, Barrow, Southport, and Workington, often appear in separate sections on dealers' lists and are quite sought-after by some collectors. Similarly, programmes from clubs' first and last seasons in the league, especially issues for the very first or last matches, are very collectable, although not always particularly rare.

Many of the early cup final programmes are eagerly sought-after by collectors, notably such issues as the 1923 FA Cup Final, and other rare pre-war offerings. Big match programmes are, however, often devalued by massive issues and subsequent reprints. This is particularly true of modern-day cup final issues. Sell-out games can increase the value of any programme, providing it is not reprinted at a future date.

Other, diverse, reasons for increased value of programmes include special occasions, such as a visit from Royalty, or tragedies, such as the 1957/8 Munich air disaster involving Manchester United, or the more recent Bradford fire disaster.

Questions such as, 'Was there really a programme issued or not?' for a match, generally stem from the inclement weather conditions of the period concerned. Frequently, programmes are prepared for matches, only for bad weather to cause numerous postponements and to outdate such issues. The decision then has to be taken whether to issue the original programme, re-issue with a supplement, or destroy and issue a totally new programme.

Collectors often find that postponed issues are available on the market, and face something of a dilemma, as they try to decide whether or not to bother purchasing items for what, in reality, are non-existent matches. Availability of such items varies enormously, depending upon the clubs involved, and the decision by printers whether to release or destroy such items. Postponed issues that are available on the market do also vary considerably in price, but generally fall into one of five categories:

1. **Advertisers' copies.** The first few copies of a print run, for advertisers and programme editors, are often sent even when no programmes reach the home club. There are generally very small quantities involved, and consequently, these are very rare.
2. **Postal Subscribers' copies.** Varies between clubs, but subscribers usually have preference over the general public, and numbers fluctuate according to the support and size of the subscription list.
3. **Club shop retained copies.** Some printers are happy to leave several hundred copies to be sold by the club, while the rest are destroyed. Variations in quantities are due to many clubs being unwilling to take the risk of trying to sell stock for a match that was never played.
4. **Wholesale issues.** Wholesale purchasing by shops or dealers of several thousand copies of postponed match programmes that would otherwise be scrapped, can mean that many copies are on the market at reasonable prices.
5. **Miscellaneous issues.** Generally obtained through contacts with, or at, printers, who retain a few copies from the quantity that are destroyed. Again, very rare.

A good example of a rare issue is the programme for the Carlisle v. Middlesbrough league match of 27 January 1973. On the Friday evening, there was a fire at the printers, who decided that the programmes were too badly damaged and should subsequently be destroyed. No programmes were available for sale on the day of the match, but some of the printer's employees salvaged a few copies, some of which have subsequently appeared on the market.

Another example of a rare and unusual programme is the 1939/40 double issue prepared for Stockport Reserves v. Northwich Victoria, Saturday 2 September 1939 and Stockport v. Doncaster, Division 3 North, Monday 4 September 1939.

Although the reserve team fixture was played, war was declared on Sunday and the first team fixture never took place.

Some collectors have been dismayed at the soaring prices of many of the rarer items within the hobby. Scan any of the larger dealers' offers lists, however, and you will find a fascinating array of programmes, all sought-after for different reasons, whether they be old, rare, unique, or purely of some special interest. Most will indeed be expensive, but none will be sold unless the collector is agreeable with (or resigned to) the prices payable.

3
The Hobby

hobby ('hɒbɪ)*n.*, *pl.* **-bies**   an activity
pursued in spare time for pleasure or
relaxation.

The Hobby

The hobby of football programme collecting, whilst arguably in existence from the days of the very first issues of the 19th Century, has only really developed in the last 25 years. In this respect, it is still in its infancy compared with other collecting hobbies. Indeed, one has only to browse through the shelves of large newsagents and booksellers to see the vast range of publications devoted to stamps, coins, postcards, and antiques. Very few will stock publications about football programmes, although there are currently two monthly magazines in circulation.

Collecting football programmes really differs from other collecting hobbies in subject matter only, and the success of the hobby is hardly surprising, given the huge interest in soccer around the world.

Football programmes greatly reflect the changing face of football through the years. In this respect, it is a dynamic hobby, responding and shaping itself to fluctuations within the sport to meet the continued demands of the spectator. Recent disasters like the 1985 Bradford and Brussels tragedies, which have directly affected the sport of football, have also had secondary effects on programme collecting. The immediate impact of the European ban was to restrict the availability of issues to collectors of British clubs in Europe, whilst the Bradford disaster resulted in a range of fund raising attempts throughout the hobby. Whilst football has shaken under the full impact of these disasters, collecting has emerged with credit and remains essentially a friendly hobby.

A vast variety of fascinating issues are available, and the hobby has gradually adopted a more professional approach, with a trade association for dealers, large numbers of well organised fairs, and increased numbers of dealers and programme clubs. All these factors not only make access to the hobby much easier, but have also considerably developed the commercial aspects of collecting.

The collector is faced with a wide choice of collecting categories. Whilst many enthusiasts collect the programmes of their favourite team, the emphasis has switched in recent years to non-league football, where the choice and variety of programmes is wider than ever and smaller clubs are only now capitalising on the commercial potential of the match day programme. Non-league issues also tend to be considerably cheaper (and frequently more informative) than their Football League competitors. This growth of the hobby at 'grass-roots' level bodes well for the future of programme collecting.

The potential of the football programme has not gone unnoticed by league clubs, and most issues today are high quality, colour, glossy, and informative publications. Prices have also risen dramatically from a steady 15/20p in the mid-1970's to 40p, 50p, and now even £1 for standard league issues. Distribution of programmes in general has greatly improved. Cup Final programmes, for example, are now available at most newsagents well before the day of the match.

Like all collecting hobbies, it can be addictive, and the majority of football programme collectors intend to continue collecting indefinitely. It has an obvious attraction to all football fans, in that a programme collection represents a fascinating history of the sport. The memorable matches of favourite teams are preserved in print to be read at a future date. Nostalgia plays an important part in most collecting hobbies, and football in particular.

The hobby is certainly not just for the younger enthusiast; indeed, concern has been expressed at the declining numbers of young collectors now entering the hobby. When programme collecting was still in its infancy, early traders, whilst perhaps less professional than their modern-day counterparts, had a certain empathy with young collectors. Attractive marketing and cheap programmes attracted many youngsters, who today form the core of the experienced collectors. Rising prices and more vigorous commercial attitudes, poor marketing, and a basic short-sightedness within the hobby, account for the present lack of appeal to younger collectors. Nevertheless, the hobby continues to expand.

Programme collecting is a hobby that can fit any pocket; vast sums can be spent on purchasing rare and historic issues or purchases can be restricted within a small budget to common issues. Most programmes from the 1960's to present date can be obtained at a very modest cost.

Collecting need not be a lonely hobby either; the growing number of programme clubs, and increased 'network' of collectors, has led to improved communications within collecting circles. There are now many opportunities to make contact with other collectors. It is also a truly international hobby, and collectors have the opportunity to exchange and correspond with other enthusiasts world-wide.

For many collectors, the hobby begins with programmes from the first matches attended, or with gifts from friends or relatives, and from there the collection just grows . . .

Trade Associations and Organisations

As a hobby or profession develops, a growing number of important bodies and organisations within the trade will be formed. The pastime of collecting football programmes is no exception. Although the organisations detailed in this chapter are probably the best known in the hobby, there are numerous programme clubs and small collectors' clubs that are also worthy of a mention. Many of these smaller organisations are affiliated to Football League clubs, or their supporters' clubs, and frequently specialise in specific categories of programmes. Indeed, the trend seems to be heading towards more of these small, specialised organisations.

Much discussion within the hobby has been devoted to the subject of the formation of a National Programme Club. Such a club would aim to help collectors throughout the world to stay in touch with each other and the hobby, encourage newcomers, act as a source of information for collectors, and aim to market the hobby to the general public. Of particular importance would be the role of cultivating a growing number of young collectors, who are, of course, the mainstay of the hobby, being the keen collectors and club organisers of future years. Existing bodies within the hobby have been criticised for placing too much emphasis upon commerce and self-interest, which is a rather short-sighted attitude, bearing in mind that future trade depends upon newcomers to collecting.

A National Programme Club would need to be self-financed, non-commercial, and would presumably require a full-time Secretary. This person would need to be able and willing to attend to numerous daily enquiries and problems, and preferably be experienced as well as enthusiastic.

While the politics of business leave increasingly less time

for the niceties of friendship, exchanges, and free information, a National Programme Club could draw upon the strengths of the essentially friendly and unselfish majority of supporters and collectors in the hobby.

The founder of any such organisation would do well to study the pitfalls and successes of past and present organisations.

The British Programme Collectors Club

The BPCC originated in Hull in 1961, and aimed initially to encourage local Cubs and Scouts to collect football programmes! The first meeting was held in a local church hall, with a few dozen spare copies of various programmes being given away by the founder of the BPCC, Norman Lovett. Such was the enthusiasm displayed for the hobby, that plans were made to form a football programme collectors' club.

The Hull Programme Club, as it was then named, attempted to go national after several successful months, and an advertisement was placed in 'Soccer Star' magazine. Foreseen as being a purely part-time venture, run for pleasure and not profit, the club was inundated with applications, with over 1,000 members enrolling in a short space of time. Unable to cope with this unprecedented volume of business, it soon became a victim of its own success, and folded shortly thereafter.

Plans to reform the full-time club began on a small scale in 1966, with the opening of a programme shop in Hull. In October 1967, the club was relaunched nationally, with a greatly restricted membership of only two hundred. This limit was increased to three hundred in due course, and again in 1973, to the maximum four hundred.

The club's failure to cater for the majority of collectors, its 'specialist' image, and its over-commercial viewpoint of the hobby (for example, members-only postal auctions of very rare items, and special purchasing rates), were criticised by many. It should be remembered, however, that the BPCC pioneered much of the early development of the hobby, notably through the introduction of postal auctions, monthly programme bulletins, and the first Programme Awards in 1965.

It was also responsible for bringing the hobby of programme collecting to the television screen, for the first 'live' programme auction, held in London, and produced the first 'Football Programme Collectors Handbook'.

The Football Programme Directory

Editor: David Stacey, 66 Southend Road, Wickford, Essex SS11 8EN
Partners: David Stacey, David Jennings, Bernard Chaplin
Annual Subscription: UK £6, Overseas £7 issued monthly
Approximate Circulation: 800

The FPD was founded in 1974 by the Revd. David Wiseman, who was also the first editor of the magazine.

Formed under the motto 'co-operation and friendship', the FPD aims to promote and further the interests of the hobby amongst collectors. It endeavours to be a link between programmes and collecting, and sets out to attract football followers from around the world.

The organisation is run on a voluntary basis, and does not aim to compete with programme clubs or dealers. Indeed, organisers and members of such clubs, and dealers themselves, are always welcome to join. Membership is worldwide, with collectors from as far afield as Canada, Mauritius, and America. Of the original membership in November 1974 (which then totalled 79), two-thirds are still members and remain committed to the hobby.

The FPD issue a monthly magazine, and members, who are invited to contribute articles for publication, have an opportunity to advertise cheaply through its pages. The magazine contains articles, letters, exchanges, features, and adverts, and lists new members and their collecting interests. The emphasis is placed firmly upon friendship throughout the footballing world, and members are asked to promote 'goodwill and interest amongst collectors'.

The partners of the FPD all have a keen interest in the

game, as well as being very much involved with football programmes. They do, however, reserve the right to cancel membership if the conduct of a member warrants such action.

Involvement with football clubs and supporters' associations, in the organisation of programme fairs, is a further role of the FPD. This activity culminates in the highlight of the FPD year, the organisation of the International Football Programme Fair. This event is the largest fair in the football programme world, and is held each June at a London venue. One partner of the FPD, David Jennings, also hosts the monthly meetings of the Southern Area of Football Programme Collectors, on the first Thursday of each month, in London. With a friendly but professional attitude, the aims of the organisation are beyond reproach, and membership continues to grow.

Programme Monthly

Editor: John Litster, 14 Raith Crescent, Kirkaldy, Fife KY2 5NN
Annual Subscription: UK £12 issued monthly
Approximate Circulation: 2,000

The most popular magazine in the hobby was born from 'Scottish Programme Review', a monthly publication published by John Litster between 1977 and 1979, with a pronounced and deliberate Scottish bias. In late 1980 Peter Butcher aided the launch of the national programme magazine, and in February 1981 the first issue of 'Programme Monthly' was published, with a print run of 750.

By the magazine's first birthday, the circulation had built up to a healthy 1,500. There was little room for complacency, however. The printing and presentation were rudimentary, to say the least, while some months the contents were determined by what articles and features the editor could dream up himself.

There were numerous obstacles to overcome in that first year. Pressure of work caused Peter Butcher to drop out after half a dozen issues; there were a couple of occasions, early on, when publishing deadlines were not met, which resulted in a double issue over two months, and a gap of one summer month. Criticism was met in the hobby, with some competitors not too appreciative of some biting wit, and concerned that age old practices were being exposed and criticised.

Although 'Programme Monthly' had its faults, it had the great benefit of being a 'stayer', and it took the best part of three years before the magazine achieved real stability and recognition within the trade. It was instrumental in the formation of the Trade Association 'PACT', and continued its quest to expose dubious practices among dealers and collectors.

The magazine began to feed off its own success, with more and more collectors subscribing to it, contributing news and information, and using its pages as a medium to advertise their sales and wants.

The presentation kept apace, with a change of printers in 1984 bringing new dimensions to the magazine, culminating in the introduction of full colour covers in 1985. The number of pages also increased, and today as many as 40 pages of pure content are included in each issue.

The purpose of the magazine remains the same. 'Programme Monthly' exists to inform, entertain, and advise. Readers around the world are urged to write in with news of programmes and programme matters in their locality. Regular columnists share their accumulated knowledge with collectors, and several series explore old, interesting, and bizarre programme issues.

With a constant desire to improve the publication in terms of size, standard of content, presentation, and distribution, every effort is made on the part of the editor towards this end. Ultimately, however, the success of 'Programme Monthly' lies in the hands of its readers.

The Association of Football Statisticians

Editor/Publisher: Ray Spiller, 22 Bretons, Basildon, Essex SS15 5BY
Annual Subscription: £7.20 (payable May) includes 6 issues and free use of library
Approximate Circulation: 1,450

How easy it is to obtain the statistics of cricket. There have been hundreds of books detailing the game's history and recording just about every ball that's been bowled since the mid-19th century. Up until recently, however, the same could not be said of football.

Football, *the* world game, was attracting a growing army of historians, record-keepers, and statisticians, all eager to gather information about their teams or interests.

It was apparent that the sport required a network of people with the mutual interest of maintaining and developing records about clubs and players. Thus, in July 1978, the Association of Football Statisticians (AFS) was formed by Ray Spiller, to fulfil what was seen as a real need.

Since that time, the quantity and quality of information available through the AFS network has been greatly improved, and membership has shown remarkable growth.

From the handful of UK enthusiasts which started the AFS, membership has grown to over 1,400 members, living in 33 different countries around the world (including Russia, Hong Kong, New Zealand, Argentina, and Turkey).

The AFS also publishes books of interest to the football statistician, and aims in particular to publish previously unreleased material. Publications have included subjects such as the birth of the Football League, details of the Scottish Football

Association, and information on the World Cup, FA Cup, Non-league, and Irish football.

The AFS uses a number of people to compile statistics for its own library, which contains more than two thousand books and magazines, and masses of information about football. Access to the library for members is by appointment, and a photocopy and information exchange system is also operated.

Among the other benefits available to members, are the publication of a bi-monthly magazine, a cross-indexed membership register, regular meetings arranged throughout the UK, and information about new publications as they are produced. Statistical contributions for publications are always welcome, although the AFS cannot guarantee that they will always be published.

The Association's aims include the fostering of friendship among fans, and the AFS has the full approval of the Football Association and the Football Leagues of both England and Scotland. It has also attracted the attention of the media, and has received numerous acknowledgements for providing information for television, radio and newspaper.

The Programme Association for Collectors and Traders

The Programme Dealers' Association was formed in 1980, by former British Programme Club secretary Norman Lovett. Unfortunately, it transpired that too few of the original members genuinely believed in the need for a trade organisation, and the PDA was shortlived and achieved little.

Faced with losses by many collectors, and with several unscrupulous dealers in operation, the magazine 'Programme Monthly' advocated the need for an effective trade protection organisation:

'. . . a start has been made by the PDA, much criticised for its apparent inactivity in the face of . . . transgressions by dealers and collectors. The PDA is a move in the right direction, however, and one which could be built upon towards the consensus view of what is good for the hobby for dealer and collector alike.

'The lead has to come from the top of the hobby, and that means prominent dealers. While the strongest trade organisation in the world cannot prevent fraudulent dealing outside of its sphere of influence, it could at least provide guaranteed indemnity against loss at the hands of a member, and a cast-iron guarantee that those on its membership are reputable dealers'.

On 4 February 1982, Roy Calmels convened a meeting of Southern dealers, and the Programme Association for Collectors and Traders (PACT) was born. Initially established in the Southern area, it was hoped to encourage dealers elsewhere in the country to follow the lead, and thereby build a national trade organisation.

The first year of PACT ran smoothly. Experienced dealers and collectors met, discussed, and then formed guidelines that were wholly for the good of the hobby. There could be few arguments, either, with the aims and objectives of the organisation:

(i) The protection and assistance of members and their clients.
(ii) The provision of a service for the arbitration of disputes.
(iii) The provision of a platform for the discussion of topics concerning football programme collecting.

At the start of the 1984/5 season, some market research was undertaken by PACT, and a series of guidelines on aspects such as offers sections/postal auctions were prepared. These have proved to be extremely useful to the hobby, and remain the best source of reference for collectors and dealers alike. The organisation has also been instrumental in solving many disputes and problems between dealers and collectors.

The jobs of running the organisation involve a great deal of time; those who participate, do so primarily as a labour of love, and devote a significant amount of time to the development of the hobby. Collectors and enthusiasts in the football programme world would do well to remember this fact, even if they are reticent in acknowledging it.

Apathy is always a powerful enemy to overcome, but those involved with the development of PACT remain optimistic. The organisation definitely has a role to play, and remains the best court of appeal for problems within the hobby. It is hoped that those who prefer to steer well clear of trade associations will at least conduct their affairs, within PACT guidelines, in a manner which will serve their clients, serve the hobby, and encourage new collectors.

The Hobby Abroad

While most clubs in Britain, at all levels, issue some form of match day programme, issues abroad vary enormously in style and availability. It is probably these aspects that make collecting foreign programmes so challenging, interesting, and rewarding. Many programmes on the continent are sponsored by advertisers, and are printed only for league games, with few issues for friendlies or European matches. In addition, the style and format of foreign programmes often reflect the difference in structure of leagues and clubs between countries, as well as the importance of the sport of football within those countries.

Although some countries are now realising the potential of programmes, outside of the UK and Scandinavia, interest in the hobby of programme collecting is still minimal. In some countries, programmes are rarely issued, even for important games, and the quality of paper and print frequently leaves much to be desired.

Obtaining programmes from abroad can prove to be difficult, and sometimes expensive. Even with the improvements in international communications experienced in recent years, ordering programmes from abroad can occasionally prove impossible for even the most persistent dealer. In such cases, returning supporters and collectors from abroad are often the only source of programmes, subsequently making them extremely rare. Where larger clubs are involved, and demand is high, prices can prove too expensive for many collectors.

Despite the possibility of ordering problems, programmes can still be obtained at minimal cost from many countries, notably in Scandinavia, where interest in programme collecting, and the British soccer scene in general, is high. There are a few UK dealers who specialise in importing foreign programmes, and also foreign programme clubs and dealers, who can offer match programmes involving British clubs at reasonable prices, even allowing for higher postage costs.

One note of caution, however; enjoyment can be limited by a failure to understand a single printed word of some foreign issues!

In **Albania**, no match programmes are issued for any fixtures, although club details are printed in newspapers. Some club publications are issued, containing squads and fixture details.

Visits of clubs to **Australia** usually result in two different programme issues. If the visiting team plays in most states, and also against the Australian representative team, then the Australian FA produces an official tour brochure to cover all these games. Usually, the individual states also issue official programmes for the matches in which they are involved. International and World Cup match programmes are issued, although in some cases a single programme will cover a series of matches.

Standard **Austrian** International issues are good value, with a usual 40 pages, colour cover, numerous black and white photographs, plenty of reading material, and only a few pages of advertisements.

The programme trend in **Belgium** reflects the fact that most Belgian clubs consist not only of a large number of separate teams of varying ages, but also of several different sports. Match day publications are usually club magazines which give news of the different teams within the club. A match day is simply regarded as being an opportune moment to distribute such a publication to the public. Consequently, programmes are not usually issued for friendlies or cup matches, although there are regular league issues.

Programmes often adopt the large, newspaper-style format, with a high proportion of advertising space, although a few clubs issue 'regular' size publications. In some cases, the club magazine is not issued at all on match days, but is distributed during the week through the letter boxes of local residents.

This can make it almost impossible for visiting supporters, arriving on the day of the match, to obtain a copy.

Prices are generally quite low, depending upon advertising content, with some issues enjoying free distribution. Less wealthy clubs often issue monthly, or even bi-monthly magazines. Even Internationals and Cup matches are prone to the eccentricities of the Belgian programme trade, and few people can predict whether a programme will appear or not!

Very few programmes are issued in **Bulgaria**, although occasional International programmes are produced. Some clubs do publish handbooks to cover the whole season, containing statistics, fixtures and squad details.

Programmes in **Czechoslovakia** contain plenty of information, but are generally printed on poor quality, thin paper, or presented in newspaper style.

In common with most Scandinavian countries, programmes are issued for the majority of league, cup and International matches in **Denmark**. Most are glossy issues with numerous advertisements and usually black and white photographs. The hobby of programme collecting in Scandinavia may not be on the same scale as in Britain, but there are several established dealers in the trade, and many enthusiasts who correspond regularly with their British counterparts.

Most clubs in **Finland** do not issue programmes for individual league fixtures, but instead produce handbooks at the start of each season. These contain fixtures, pen-pictures of players, squad numbers and details of players from other clubs. Of the few programmes that are produced for individual matches, many are either newspaper format or large single-sheet issues.

East German issues are quite different from the productions of their Western neighbours; usually small format, informative programmes of 8 pages, on glossy paper, with occasional black and white photographs.

In **West Germany**, very few clubs published programmes until the formation of the Bundesliga (Premier Division) in 1963, although 'Die Blaue' ('The Blue One') issue of Bayern

Munich and TSV 1860 Munich, was established far back in 1922. This programme still retains its traditional image and has remained almost unchanged in format since its publication. Most early issues were, and some modern issues still are, produced by private companies or individuals. Older programmes frequently used the newspaper format, while today's glossy, full-colour issues are usually much smaller in size.

Programmes are issued, with very few exceptions, for all today's league games, but confusion can arise when as many as four or five different 'Official' programmes and magazines are available at the same ground. Issues for friendlies and European ties are less common, as many programmes are sponsored by advertisers, who have no agreement covering such matches.

Clubs in **Greece** do not issue programmes as such, preferring weekly club newspapers, although programmes have been issued (usually free of charge) for some European and International matches.

In **Holland**, the majority of league and top non-league clubs all issue programmes, with a wide variety in style, format and content. Most issues carry a large amount of advertising and usually contain numerous black and white photographs. Newspaper editions still remain popular with some clubs. Programmes should not be confused with the club magazines that frequently appear at matches, and which can easily be mistaken for match day programmes by over-enthusiastic overseas visitors.

League programmes are very rare in **Hungary**, most clubs preferring to issue magazines covering all sports within the club.

Programmes are also uncommon in **Iceland**, although generally containing interesting reading material in otherwise poor quality black and white offerings.

Sports programmes as a whole are not difficult to obtain in **Israel**, but football programmes are quite rare. League programmes are almost non-existent, and little interest is shown by the public in the few issues that are produced. With five divisions and 250 clubs, the footballing public often has difficulty in identifying opposition team players, who can quite frequently remain anonymous throughout an entire match!

Even for cup finals, very few programmes exist, although friendly matches with British clubs have resulted in some interesting issues, frequently packed with advertisements. International programmes are usually issued, although both style and content tend to be disappointing, and information is frequently dated.

Football programmes, as such, do not exist in **Italy**. Instead, the public are faced with a continuous deluge of daily sports papers, and, reading about football events each day, are usually well prepared for the matches that they attend!

Pre-match newspapers issued are often large format single-sheets with numerous advertisements and little information. Several private publishing companies have attempted to market club magazines, but even the best of these issues, such as 'Roma mia', and 'Juventus FC', barely reach the standard of current English fourth division publications. Neither are they 'official' issues in many cases, as they are produced without being sanctioned by the clubs involved. Even for official Big Matches, such as European Cup Finals, much confusion surrounds the issue of many different, usually unofficial, publications that are available at, and before, the game. Perhaps it is not surprising that programme collectors in Italy are few and far between . . .

Programmes from the Far East are rare indeed, although in **Japan**, they are invariably issued for visits of foreign clubs.

In **Malta** too, programmes are usually issued for visits of foreign clubs. With considerable interest in British soccer on this small island, more substantial programmes, with black and white photographs and interesting reading material, usually accompany the visit of a British club.

Norwegian programmes usually have many pages but, in common with most Scandinavian issues, contain only limited reading material and a large proportion of advertisements.

Poland has suffered more than its fair share of economic difficulties in recent years, and this is reflected in the rather drab and dull issues that are produced. Programmes are frequently thin card covers with limited contents and restricted print-runs. Some excellent international programmes, however, have been produced, with plenty of reading material and the occasional black and white photograph.

In **Portugal**, programmes are not normally issued for any matches. Programmes in **Rumania** are usually poor quality, large-format sheets, folded two or three times and without photographs.

Russia, unlike other Eastern European countries, where programme issues are usually vague and irregular, produces programmes for all important matches. The standard format is an 8" × 5", four-page issue, or a single sheet folded three or four times, although more glossy issues have been produced for some games. Most Russian programme covers are very colourful, and frequently, programmes for the same match will have several different cover designs. There is usually plenty of reading material, with occasional black and white photographs in larger offerings. Not all programmes give match details or line-ups, but all at least provide a preview of the game involved.

Recent years have seen an improvement in the overall quality of publications, with the introduction of colour photographs in some cases. Print-runs bear little direct relationship to expected attendances, particularly for Big Matches, where production of as few as 10,000 programmes for a 70,000 crowd is not unusual. The Soviet State controls the printing of all official literature, including football programmes, and printers are obliged to reveal the print quantity for any given issue. Programmes are frequently numbered to assist in this control.

Programmes in **Sweden** usually vary from 30 to 96 pages in size, with numerous advertisements, rather limited reading material, and colour covers, but only rarely with colour photographs inside. Programmes are issued for most games and productions for Big Matches are usually of a high standard.

Switzerland normally issues substantial International programmes of forty pages or more, with a few black and white photographs, numerous advertisements, and some interesting content.

In the **USA**, there is considerable interest in sports collecting, but soccer plays a poor relation to the major sports of Baseball, American Football and Hockey, with little interest in football programme collecting as a consequence.

International match programmes in **Yugoslavia** tend to contain numerous black and white photographs and few advertisements, but remain of limited quality.

The **World Cup** usually sees the production of programmes from countries that would not normally produce them, from as far afield as Africa, Asia and the Middle East.

Football is a truly international sport, and friendship often extends through the barriers that politics and business sometimes erect. A collection of foreign programmes, with their contrast in style, content, language and culture, reveals a fascinating panorama of the game's history.

4
The Collector

collector (kə'lɛtə) *n.* a person who collects or amasses objects as a hobby.

Why Collect?

Most of us have collected at some stage in our lives, whether toy soldiers, coins, stamps, medals or parking tickets! The collector, however, is still viewed by many as being a social outcast, and generally something of an oddity!

There is no collective noun for programme collectors, although the term 'programologist' is often used in collecting circles. Estimates as to the number of collectors in the UK vary considerably. Some set the level at 2,000 collectors, while others believe that as many as 20,000 collectors exist, the main reason for this discrepancy being the different statistical sources used. An estimate based upon sales of programmes around clubs in the UK would be considerably higher, for example, than one based upon the circulation of programme publications within the hobby. Nevertheless, a large number of people, mainly keen football supporters, do purchase, read, and retain, copies of match day football programmes.

The majority of enthusiasts collect current season home programmes of their favourite teams, and at least half actually attend these matches. It is also estimated that one third of all collectors watch non-league football at some level. Numbers are spread quite evenly amongst occupations, and approximately 90% of all programme collectors are male.

So much for statistics, but just what is this fascination with football programmes? What is it that makes people start collecting and why is the hobby so addictive?

Youngsters are no doubt drawn by the colour photographs of their favourite players, and the variety of sizes, colours, and designs of programmes. Older collectors are lured perhaps by nostalgia, a love of the game of football, and a fascination with its past. Collecting football programmes is a fascinating hobby, there is an enormous variety of issues available, and an immediate visual impression is gained when viewing a collection. Covers identify league clubs of different eras, and provide a geography lesson for all, as well as being of historical interest. Collecting may appear to be a hobby for the younger supporter, but recent years have seen a tremendous growth within a hobby that now has thousands of enthusiasts, both young and old, throughout the world. Like most collecting hobbies, it is a ceaseless search for the unobtainable; a completed part, or whole, of a collection being a particular source of satisfaction.

Reasons for collecting are diverse; there is the natural desire to accumulate, or an interest in a particular team, historical significance, or perhaps a personal involvement with the sport. If you have a genuine feeling and enthusiasm for the game, how can you resist browsing through programmes from seasons past? For many, this represents the true joy of collecting, delving into the past, discovering fascinating facts and articles, and evoking waves of nostalgia . . .

Every programme tells a story. Every collection is your own soccer encyclopedia. Over the years, millions of football programmes have been printed, bought, read and discarded. Public libraries and museums have many collections of rare memorabilia, but much of early football history, in the shape of old, rare, and valuable programme collections, lies in private hands.

For some, a growing collection may be the only remaining link with the sport, as many supporters abandon the terraces for the comfort of their own homes. Modest, regular sums of money, a realistic attitude, and a basic love of the game itself, is all that is needed to gain tremendous enjoyment from the hobby. You need not be rich to be a serious collector, and a serious collector can have fun without being an investor. Indeed, very few collectors buy purely for investment and sale for future profit, while the vast majority of collectors intend to carry on collecting indefinitely!

Although the cost of current season programmes has risen sharply in recent years (with few relative changes in content or format), a collection dating back twenty-five years can still be obtained at little cost.

The collector today is faced with increased standards of programme production, and more diversity (particularly through the growth of non-league programme production) than ever before. The utility of the programme varies from informative (team line-ups, fixtures, statistics), to entertaining (pre-match, half-time or post-match reading), through to its role as souvenir of the match. It should always be remembered, however, that the majority of programme buyers go to matches, first and foremost, to watch football. If a programme is issued, good. If not, then collectors have to accept that there is no programme available. Many clubs remain sporadic issuers of programmes and collecting such items, whilst rewarding, can be very frustrating. Programme buying tends to become habit-forming, but while the pros and cons of collecting can be debated at length, the onus remains with clubs to produce interesting, informative, and entertaining programmes for the supporters.

How to start

Today's beginner has many advantages over the aspirant collector of the 1950's or 1960's. The hobby now has a well-established structure of dealers, clubs, societies, fairs, magazines, and other publications. Improved communications, freely available advice, and easy access to other collectors, all make avoiding the pitfalls within the hobby considerably easier.

The first decision must be to choose the category or type of programme that you wish to collect, so that you can plan where to store items, how much to spend on them, and where best to obtain them. Many collectors start by collecting programmes of their favourite team. Although there is a wide range of choices, it is best to specialise to begin with, as interest can quickly wane under the burden of an over-optimistic collector's desires. Similarly, buying at random will soon lose its appeal, and your collection will have little form or continuity. Collectors choose programmes that relate to their favourite player, to grounds visited, or even to particular dates, such as their birth day or year. The choice is endless!

Here are some of the categories that you may wish to collect:

Big Match
Very popular, usually easily available and relatively cheap. Includes:
FA Cup Finals.
League/Milk/Littlewoods Cup Finals.
FA Charity Shield.
European Finals (UEFA, European and European Cup Winners Cups).
European Championship Finals.
World Cup Finals.
Cup semi-finals.

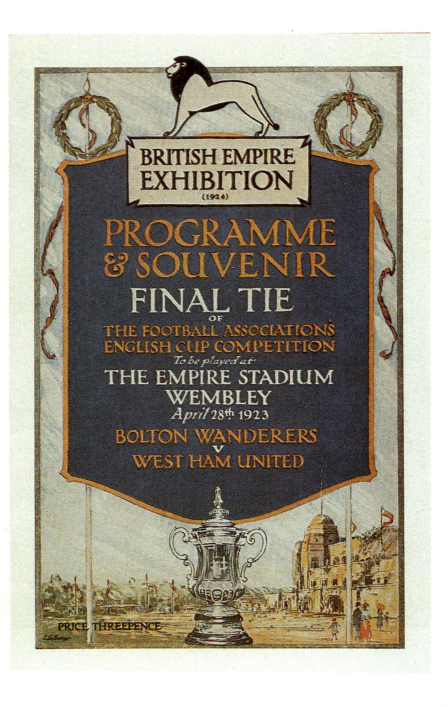

In 1923, Bolton Wanderers defeated West Ham United 2–0 in the first Wembley FA Cup Final. The programme for this match is now one of the most prized possessions in the hobby.

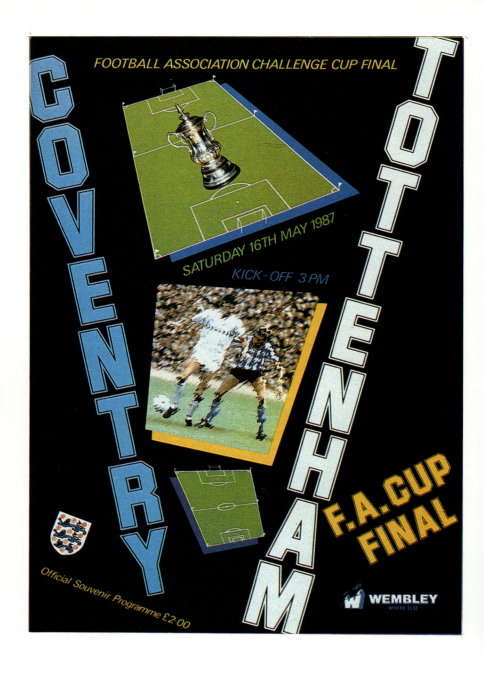

The 1987 FA Cup Final displays the glossy, large-size Wembley programme style of the 1980's. Success here at last for Coventry City — after 94 years as a professional club.

The CHELSEA F.C. Chronicle

OFFICIAL PROGRAMME

of

The Chelsea Football & Athletic Company, Limited.

MEMBERS OF THE FOOTBALL LEAGUE (Second Division).
The London Football Combination.
Runners-up—FOOTBALL ASSOCIATION CUP 1914—1915.

Vol. XXI. No. 47.   Saturday, 24th April, 1926.   TWOPENCE.
POST FREE 3D.

REFLECTIONS ON THE SEASON'S PLAY.

The Pensioner always game.   By Charles Shaw Baker.

*'The Chelsea Chronicle' for the 1925/6 Division Two match with Middlesbrough provides
a classic example of a pre-war programme.*

Tottenham Hotspur Football & Athletic Company, Limited

Official Programme

And Record of the Club.

Issued every Match Day. **PRICE ONE PENNY.**

VOL. XXX, No. 41. FEBRUARY 26, 1938.

THE FAMOUS CLUB HOUSE AT CRAVEN COTTAGE WHERE BULWER LYTTON WROTE — "THE LAST DAYS OF POMPEII."

THERE IS NO FEAR OF CRAVEN COTTAGE 'GOING TO RUINS' WHILE MR DEAN IS IN THE CHAIR

AND AS BILL VOISEY IS IN CHARGE OF THE TRAINING THERE ARE NO OLD CROCKS EITHER.

Crusha & Son., Ltd., Tottenham, Enfield, Palmers Green and Wood Green.

Cartoons were very popular in many pre-war club issues, as shown by this 1937/8 Tottenham programme.

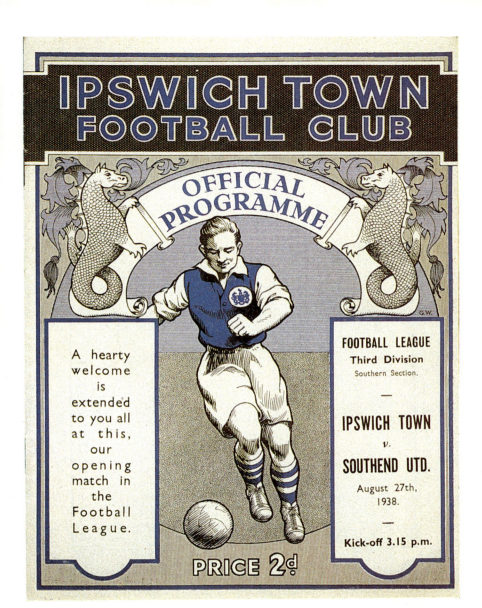

IPSWICH TOWN
FOOTBALL CLUB

OFFICIAL PROGRAMME

A hearty welcome is extended to you all at this, our opening match in the Football League.

FOOTBALL LEAGUE

Third Division

Southern Section.

—

IPSWICH TOWN

v.

SOUTHEND UTD.

August 27th, 1938.

—

Kick-off 3.15 p.m.

PRICE 2ᵈ

Ipswich Town entered the Football League in 1938/9 and defeated Southend United 4–2 in their first game of the season.

CHARLTON ATHLETIC

Vol. XIV—No. 5 | SATURDAY, SEPT. 21st, 1946 | Price 2d.

CHARLTON
v.
SHEFFIELD UNITED

CLUB NOTES by Charltonian

"NAP" HAND AGAINST SUNDERLAND.

After the indifferent showing against Manchester United a good win was needed by way of atonement and that is just what happened a few days later when Sunderland, coming to the Valley with an unbeaten record, had their colours lowered by the wide margin of five clear goals.

This was truly a really great show by Charlton, yet it was a game in which our boys might well have added further goals and also the visitors might have got one or two. There were more near-misses and last-second saves in this game that one might see in a whole season. It was all very entertaining and the changes made in the composition of the team certainly strengthened the side. A three-goals lead was built up before the interval and increased to five before the end, with the visitors failing to reply. Don Welsh (2), Chris Duffy, Bill Robinson and Leslie Fell scored.

CHARLTON CONCEDE A "NAP" HAND.

After getting a "nap" hand in goals against Sunderland the topsy-turvy early season form which seems to be effecting quite a lot of clubs saw Charlton concede one. This happened at Preston, where Charlton lost 5—1 with exactly the same team that had routed Sunderland. Such a reversal of form almost beggars description but the fact remains Charlton were overplayed in rather surprising fashion at Deepdale where Preston finished very good winners.

With rain falling throughout the

(cont. on p. 3)

HOT **OXO**
so good to drink...
so easy to make

STACY & SON, LTD., LONDON, N.1.

A typical 1940's issue. Programmes from this era are not noted for their colour or variety.

BURNLEY
FOOTBALL CLUB
SEASON 1956-1957

F.A.
CUP WINNERS
1913 - 1914

F.A.
CUP FINALISTS
1946 - 1947

CHAMPIONS: Div. I, 1920-21; Central League, 1948-49; Div. II, 1897-98
RUNNERS-UP: Div. I, 1919-20; Div. II, 1912-13, 1946-47
WINNERS, LANCASHIRE CUP: 1890, 1914-15, 1949-50, 1951-52

OFFICIAL **3D** PROGRAMME
PUBLISHED BY BURNLEY FOOTBALL & ATHLETIC CO. LTD.

LEAGUE CHAMPIONS 1954-55

Chelsea
Football Club
Stamford Bridge Grounds, London SW6

FOOTBALL LEAGUE—DIVISION I SEASON 1956-57

CHELSEA
v
MANCHESTER UNITED
Wednesday, 5th September, 1956 Kick-off 6.0 p.m.

Official Programme **6d** The right of admission to grounds is reserved.

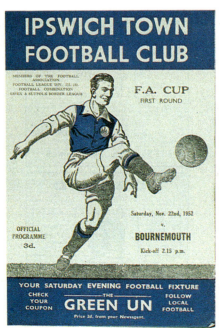

IPSWICH TOWN
FOOTBALL CLUB

MEMBERS OF THE FOOTBALL
ASSOCIATION
FOOTBALL LEAGUE DIV. III. (S)
FOOTBALL COMBINATION
ESSEX & SUFFOLK BORDER LEAGUE

F.A. CUP
FIRST ROUND

Saturday, Nov. 22nd, 1952
v.
BOURNEMOUTH
Kick-off 2.15 p.m.

OFFICIAL
PROGRAMME
3d.

YOUR SATURDAY EVENING FOOTBALL FIXTURE
CHECK
YOUR
COUPON

THE
GREEN UN
Price 2d. from your Newsagent.

FOLLOW
LOCAL
FOOTBALL

PORT VALE

1876

1954-55

PORT VALE FOOTBALL CLUB

3d

Many programmes of the 1950's were similar in size, but a variety of distinctive club designs soon began to emerge.

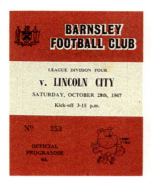
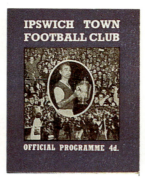
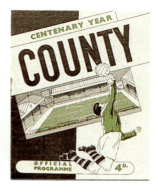
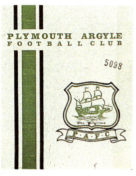

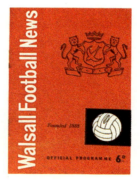

A selection of the small, pocket-sized programmes which were very popular for a period during the 1960's.

Internationals
Readily available and quite cheap. Includes:
England Homes.
England Home and Aways.
Other countries' Home and Aways.
Minor Internationals (Youth, U-21, U-23, etc.).

Minor Competitions
Generally inexpensive but not always easy to obtain. Includes:
Texaco, Willhire, Full Members, and Freight Rover trophies.

Non-league
Ever-increasing interest in the great variety and originality of these issues, which are usually inexpensive.

Specials and miscellaneous
Wide variety in prices and availability. Includes:
Friendlies and testimonials, pre-season/close-season tours.
Ex-league clubs (Accrington Stanley, Gateshead, etc.).
First and last season in the Football League.
Championship winning matches or seasons, promoted/relegated teams.
Pre-war issues, war-time issues.
Cup matches from 1st round proper.
British Clubs in Europe.
Scottish/Irish/Welsh issues.
European/continental issues.
One per club per season.

Having chosen which programmes you wish to collect, it is a good idea to prepare a checklist. This will contain a list of the programmes you require, and your own records of these items, their price, and their condition, as you acquire them. You can usually obtain such lists by reference to publications and statistical sources such as yearbooks, handbooks, and club histories. If you choose to photocopy pages from publications, do make sure that you are not infringing copyright law.

You should also have somewhere to store your programme collection. They should be protected from dust, grease, damp, and sunlight, and preferably stored flat to avoid creased and torn edges. Initially, a shoe box, binder, folder, or strong envelope, should prove adequate for your requirements.

Now you must decide how much money you are prepared to spend on your programmes. A collection should primarily be about quality, content, and interest to the collector – not monetary value. Collectors are often intent upon filling gaps in their collections in the shortest possible time, but should beware of placing too high a price upon wanted items. Regular, modest sums of money, can ensure a reasonable collection in a fairly short space of time. Despite rising prices, there are still many programmes available cheaply, and bundles of less rare items are easily available from dealers and shops. The main disadvantage of such bundles is their proportionately high postage costs.

Obtaining programmes

You will probably obtain your first football programmes from the matches that you first attend. You may, however, be unable to attend some matches, or you may find that some programmes you require have sold out.

Most league clubs now offer a subscription service, which is particularly useful if you cannot obtain programmes for the matches that you require. You can also obtain postponed issues through this service, as most programmes are sent out before the match day (and consequently before any cancellation or postponement). The programmes should arrive uncreased, but receiving items through the post will always make this element of risk difficult to eliminate.

When writing to clubs for programmes, ensure that you send sufficient remittance to cover postage costs. You may find it convenient to send a stamped addressed envelope or stamps, but ensure that any envelope you send is large enough to hold the items you are sending for. Always print your name and address clearly, and keep letters brief. Address your communication to the Club Secretary, or Programme Editor, and always state your exact requirements (see figures 4.1 and 4.2).

Never send coins through the post. Postal orders are convenient and easy to obtain, although rather expensive for large amounts. Cheques are generally safer and cheaper. If you do not have a bank account, you could ask a friend or relative to write a cheque for you.

Most club shops stock programmes from home and away matches as well as a reasonable range of Big Match issues. You can ring to reserve items in many cases, although the club may refuse to do so if the programmes are expected to sell out. If you miss a few issues from a season, try contacting the relevant supporters club, or join a programme club, many of

6 Chapter Street
Tuttenham
TW6 0TX
24th July 19–

The Programme Editor
Barchester City FC
Town Lane
Barchester
BR8 7PM

Dear Sir,

Please send me details of your match day
programme subscription costs. I enclose an
SAE for your reply.

Yours faithfully

A. Collector

Fig. 4.1

6 Chapter Street
Tuttenham
TW6 0TX
12th October 19–

The Club Chairman
Barchester City FC
Town Lane
Barchester
BR8 7PM

Dear Sir,

Please send me a copy of the Barchester
City v. Tuttenham Town match day programme
of Saturday 10th October 19–, if available.
I enclose a postal order for 60p and a
large SAE.

Thank you.

Yours faithfully

A. Collector

Fig. 4.2

```
                              6 Chapter Street
                              Tuttenham
                              TW6 0TX
                              24th October 19-
A. Programme Dealer
9 Town Street
Everpool
EC23 8NL

Dear Sir,

Please send me a copy of your latest
catalogue, and details of your wants list
service, if applicable.
I enclose 26p in stamps to cover postage
costs.

Yours faithfully

A. Collector
```

Fig. 4.3

which are affiliated to league clubs anyway, and may therefore
specialise in the programmes that you require.

Programme clubs not only give free information and
newsletters, but also give access to fellow collectors, and acknow-
ledged 'experts' within the hobby. By contacting these people,
who are usually more than willing to help new collectors,
much time and energy can be saved in searching out wanted
items. Experts can also advise upon whether certain programmes exist and their current availability. Clubs are inexpensive to join, and frequently offer discounts to members
(which means that the membership cost can be quickly re-
covered) on the lists of items for sale that they issue. You may
also be able to swap or exchange programmes with fellow
collectors through programme clubs. Exchanging items enables
you to share the hobby with others, has no costs (except,
perhaps, for postage) and can use programmes that are
superfluous to your collection.

Almost half of all first time buyers obtain their programmes from dealers in the hobby. There are many dealers to choose from throughout the UK and abroad, and the majority are reliable and honest. Some dealers have shops or stands at football grounds, while most issue lists or catalogues. These issues normally include offers of cheap bundles of programmes, which, as mentioned previously, can be an ideal source for first time buyers. Ensure, however, that you really want the programmes you send for, and that you are not ordering them merely because they appear to be a bargain.

Choosing a dealer can be difficult, and it is probably best to adopt a trial and error method, until you find a dealer who best meets the needs of your collection. Always write first and discover what type of service they can offer, what their catalogues contain, how reasonable their prices are, and how professional the dealer appears (see figure 4.3, for sample letter). Next, send for a small order and see how long it takes to arrive, note the condition of the items, whether they were sent in a protected envelope, and how helpful the dealer was. Try to list alternatives whenever possible, as some programmes do sell very quickly. Remember to state whether you require a cash refund for out of stock items, as many dealers offer credit notes instead. You will soon find a dealer with whom you can trade in complete safety, and who can supply most of your programme wants. Even if you do find such a dealer, do not be afraid to send for other dealers' catalogues, as you may be pleasantly surprised to find some of your wanted programmes at lower prices! Above all, never send large amounts of money until you are sure of the dealer; it could prove to be an expensive mistake . . .

Do not worry if you obtain the occasional faulty or damaged item from a dealer. It is impossible for them to check every single programme out of the thousands in stock, and most dealers will be happy to refund, replace, or exchange unsatisfactory orders.

Some dealers include offers supplements or postal auctions

with their catalogues. These offer a number of rare items at stated minimum prices. Collectors then send in postal bids for desired programmes, and the highest bid secures each item. It is unlikely that you will use this system until your collection has grown and you have more money available to buy rare items. Indeed, many collectors never use postal auctions because they object to the high prices that result from this system.

While rare and expensive programmes may be beyond the beginner's budget, they do provide the basis for the future 'wants list'. This is a list of the programmes that you require to fill the gaps in your collection. They are not always particularly rare or old, but may still be difficult to obtain. Many dealers offer a wants list service, where they will check your lists, and notify you if they have any of the items you require in stock. Keep your wants list as brief as possible, only list the items that you really need, and your dealer may be able to help you.

One way of obtaining rare and old issues is to attend a programme fair. These events will usually be held in your area at some stage during the year. A number of dealers will have stalls at these events, and displays and exhibitions are usually arranged. A wide variety of programmes are available, many at reduced prices, no postage costs are involved, and collectors have an opportunity to judge the condition of items for themselves. Fairs are an excellent source for first time buyers, yet very few new collectors seem to use them.

Take your checklist of programmes required with you, and a container or bag to hold items as you buy them. Restrict your purchases to items you really want. It is very easy to get carried away with so many programmes on display, so limit yourself to a strict budget. Programme fairs can provide a good day out, and are also an excellent opportunity to meet dealers and other collectors. Admission is usually very cheap.

Other sources of programmes include antique or second-hand shops, antiques and collectors fairs, specialist book shops, or even car boot sales. You may need more than a little good

71

fortune to obtain programmes in this way, however!

Take care that any programmes you receive are official issues. Pirate, reprint, and fake programmes are still in circulation, even though in smaller numbers than in days gone by. Official programmes usually have the words 'official programme' or 'official souvenir programme' on the cover, while pirate issues only state 'souvenir programme'. Pirate issues used to be a common sight, especially at big matches such as cup ties, but have become rarer in recent years, as the standard of match day issues has continued to improve. Non-league clubs are particularly susceptible to programme 'piracy', where individuals sell programmes to collectors, purely for financial gain, without the club's consent or knowledge. Generally of novelty value only to collectors, and considered worthless by most, pirate issues, although serving to increase the number of programmes available on the market, devalue the hobby by their dubious origins and methods of sale.

Some fake programmes are very difficult to spot, particularly if the original item is very rare and therefore mostly unavailable for comparison with the false issue. Others are easily distinguished as fakes by differences in paper, print, or colour quality, or by slight discrepancies in size or design.

Reprints are programmes printed long after the actual game has taken place and are usually unofficial, although official reproductions of some programmes are in circulation. All reprints should state so, clearly, in the programme, preferably on the front or back cover. Official reproductions, like that of the 1923 FA Cup Final issue, allow the collector a glimpse of a rare programme that would almost certainly never be seen otherwise. They are easy to spot, usually being of totally different paper and print quality, and stating 'official reproduction' on the cover.

Finally, do not be discouraged by comparing your meagre starting collection with the hoards of rarities belonging to experienced collectors. Most collections will have grown over several years, in line with rising salaries, and collectors will have had more time, and more opportunities, to complete chosen sets. Everyone has to begin somewhere, and today's beginner will be the expert in several years time, given sufficient patience, determination, interest and commitment.

Collector's check list no. 1
Starting up

* Choose which type of programmes you want to collect.
* Prepare a check list of programmes required.
* Ensure adequate storage.
* Store programmes flat, away from heat, damp, dust and sunlight.
* Part of the joy of collecting is to be able to display your collection; choose suitable storage to allow this, if possible.
* Never set collecting targets that are too difficult to achieve. It can be easy to become disillusioned with your new hobby in this way.
* Decide how much money you have available for your collection.
* Sources of programmes include:
  Friends and relatives
  Attending matches
  Ordering from clubs
  Club subscription service
  Club shops
  Programme clubs
  Dealers
  Programme Fairs
  Antique/Second-hand shops
  Collectors' fairs/Car boot sales, etc.
* Always try to obtain programmes in good, clean condition.
* Never send coins through the post.
* Bank notes can be sent by recorded or registered post.
* If you send a blank cheque (without the amount in words or figures completed) mark it 'a/c payee only, not negotiable' and state a maximum if possible e.g. 'not to exceed £10'.
* When comparing prices for items, check whether or not they include postage; most don't, but some do.

* Take care not to part with any money until you know exactly what you are getting and who you are dealing with.
* Always print your name and address clearly on all correspondence.
* Notify any changes of address as soon as possible.
* Remember that collecting should be enjoyable. A collection should be primarily about its quality, content and interest to the collector.

Collector's check list no. 2
Storage, care and safety of your collection

To ensure that your programmes remain in the best possible condition, it is important that you follow certain guidelines when building your collection:

* A filing cabinet, bureau or chest of drawers make an ideal home for your collection.
* Strong manilla envelopes, wallet files or shoe boxes are good storage containers for programmes.
* Use card, hardboard or plywood dividers between programme sections to keep them flat and uncreased.
* File programmes in some sort of order so that you know how to find individual items, and always try to keep them tidy.
* Try not to mix sizes of programmes too much, as large issues among smaller ones can become creased and torn.
* Always try to store programmes flat, to avoid bent, creased or torn edges.
* Take a strong envelope with you when purchasing programmes.
* The less handled your programmes are, the better. Always turn pages carefully and wash hands to avoid sweat, dirt and grease.
* Special folders, binders or cellophane envelopes are ideal for storing and viewing your collection. They also mean that programmes can be handled without fear of grease or dirt.
* Avoid damp, which can rust staples and crease or stain programmes.
* Avoid direct sunlight, which can warp, curl or fade programmes.
* Keep your collection covered to avoid dirt and dust.

* Add newspaper reports to your collection for added interest.
* Never write on or inside your programmes. If you must, use a soft pencil and write lightly and neatly.
* Do not crease or fold programmes. If possible, remove any creases immediately, and straighten out folded corners.
* Do not sellotape programmes unless absolutely necessary; it tarnishes, stains and peels away with age.
* Never punch holes in a programme.
* Do not pin or staple programmes.
* Avoid cutting pictures, or vouchers, from a programme whenever possible.
* Remove paper clips to avoid future marks.
* Most collectors agree that collections are devalued by binding.
* A soft putty rubber, obtainable from art shops, is ideal for cleaning grubby programmes. Rub gently, outwards, to avoid creasing or tearing.

Postal auctions/offers supplements

Many dealers today use postal auctions (also called offers supplements) to sell old and rare items. Using this system, programmes are listed for sale, with their condition clearly described, beside a stated minimum. Collectors then send in postal bids, on or above this minimum amount, for programmes that they require. Bids are usually cash only, or cash plus rare programme exchanges. The highest bid received by the stated closing date will secure the appropriate item. Most dealers notify only the successful clients.

The system means that the collector whose need (or, perhaps, bank balance) is the greatest, can obtain a programme that may not appear on the market again for years. The dealer, too, is content in the knowledge that he has obtained the best possible price for that particular item. This appears to be the equitable and inevitable conclusion of the market laws of supply and demand.

Postal auctions are, however, open to abuse, and have faced mounting criticism under allegations of price-fixing and gazumping. Here, favoured clients are advised of the highest bids, so that they can top them with repeated bids of their own, thus unfairly penalising *bona fide* collectors who submit postal bids.

The Programme Association for Collectors and Traders (PACT), concerned at the apparent abuse of offers supplements, laid down a series of guidelines governing the system, which both collectors and dealers would do well to study.

PACT guidelines for postal offers

These guidelines were approved at a PACT committee meeting of 25 November 1984, for use by dealers, PACT members or otherwise. Collectors may safely participate in postal auctions with dealers who advertise their adherence to these guidelines, as PACT can investigate and take action against parties claiming to use them, but doing so improperly.

1 Definition
1.1   An 'Offers list' or 'Offers section' (hereinafter termed 'auction') lists programmes for which the selling price will be determined by the highest bidder in a postal auction.

2   Presentation
2.1   A brief summary of the terms under which the auction will be conducted will precede a listing of the items to be auctioned. As a minimum requirement this should state: 'The conduct of this Offers section/list/auction (etc.) will conform with the PACT Guidelines for Postal Offers, a copy of which may be obtained from the secretary of PACT. Please enclose an SAE.'
2.2   There may then follow a summary of particular/salient points.
2.3   A closing date (and time) (expiry) for receipt of offers will be specified (e.g. first post on a certain date).
2.4   It will be stated whether offers are invited in cash, programmes, or a mixture of both.
2.5   Each item will be listed as follows:
Sequential index number; full fixture details; summary description of item's condition; minimum acceptable offer.
2.6   A full inspection, internal and external, of each item listed, will be made to ensure the accuracy of description.

2.7   A pro-forma offers form may be included, with space for index number, programme details and amount of offer.

3   Conduct of auction

3.1   Offers will be accepted only by post (i.e. in writing).

3.2   Offers will be accepted only up until the expiry date/time.

3.3   For the duration of the auction, no information with regard to other bids made will be disclosed to any bidder or potential bidder.

3.4   Offers will be filed in chronological order of receipt for the duration of the auction.

3.5   In the event of two offers of an identical value being the highest received for an item, that offer received by an earlier post will succeed.

3.6   As soon as possible after the expiry date/time, successful bids will be determined and those bidders advised by post, allowing a pre-determined period (usually 14 days) in which to send payment.

3.7   If a bidder does not remit the necessary amount within the period prescribed, the next-highest bidder will be given the option to exercise his offer, under the same terms (as in 3.6 above).

3.8   On receipt of the correct remittance, items will be despatched by recorded delivery, or, if applicable, by certificate of postage.

3.9   Dealers shall not conduct auctions for items out with their normal offers lists.

3.10   Bidders will not be permitted to alter or withdraw their offers after the expiry date/time.

3.11   If a minimum offer has been exceeded within the terms of these guidelines, and within the normal spirit of trading, the programme will be sold in the normal manner.

4   Minimum offers

4.1   A programme may not be sold if the highest bid (in cash or equivalent exchange) neither matches nor exceeds the published minimum acceptable offer.

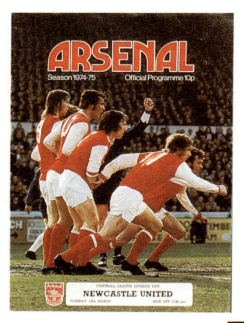

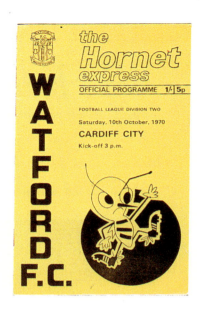

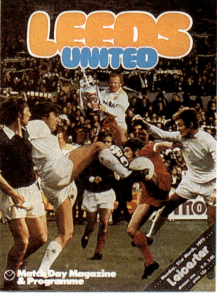

The potential of the football programme really began to be recognised in the 1970's; resulting in a wide range of improved publications.

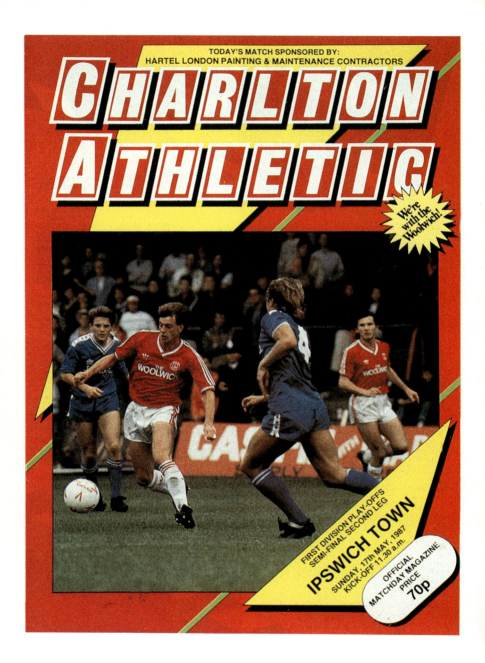

The somewhat controversial Football League promotion/relegation play-offs were introduced in the 1986/7 season. This glossy Charlton v. Ipswich issue is a typical 1980's programme.

Non-league football produces perhaps the most diverse, interesting, and unique range of all programme issues.

FOOTBALL ASSOCIATION INTERNATIONAL

ENGLAND
v
GERMANY

WEDNESDAY, DECEMBER 1st, 1954   KICK-OFF 2.0 pm

EMPIRE STADIUM

WEMBLEY

Chairman and Managing Director   SIR ARTHUR J. ELVIN, MBE
OFFICIAL PROGRAMME - ONE SHILLING

An example of the traditional Wembley programme. The style of these issues remained almost unchanged until the mid-1960's.

GATESHEAD A.F.C. Ltd.

Division IV   Saturday, November 28th, 1959

GATESHEAD v WATFORD

Official Programme   *Season*

3ð.   *1959-60*

INSIST ON THE BEST

HOGGETT'S FAMOUS PRODUCTS

(Est. 1924)

BEETROOT

PICKLED ONIONS   RED CABBAGE

PICCALILLI   VINHOGG   POMPY SAUCE

MIXED PICKLE   TOMATO KETCHUP

SILVERSKINS   MALT VINEGAR   SWEET PICKLE

Hoggett's Potato Crisps still sell at 3d. per packet

HOGGETT'S FOOD PRODUCTS LTD.

NEW MODEL FACTORY,   ASKEW ROAD WEST,   GATESHEAD

Telephone: 7-1860

A contrast in footballing fortunes in the 1959/60 season. Gateshead lost their League status, while Watford were destined for a more glamorous future.

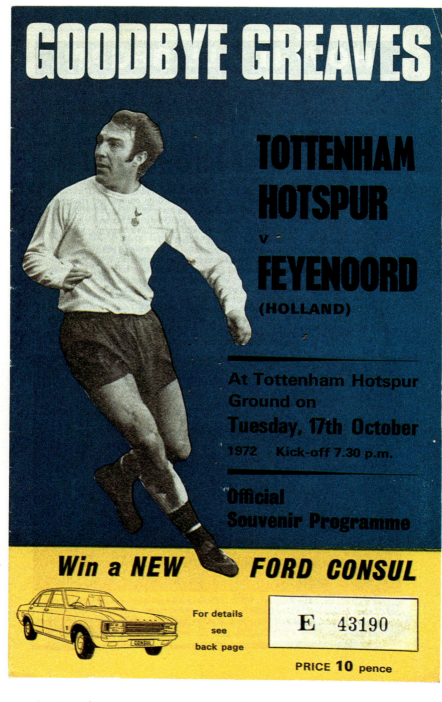

GOODBYE GREAVES

TOTTENHAM HOTSPUR
v
FEYENOORD
(HOLLAND)

At Tottenham Hotspur Ground on **Tuesday, 17th October** 1972 Kick-off 7.30 p.m.

Official Souvenir Programme

Win a NEW FORD CONSUL

For details see back page

E 43190

PRICE **10** pence

A testimonial for one of the all-time greats as Tottenham entertain Feyenoord at White Hart Lane.

'Who can stop Cruyff?' asks 'The Blue One' edition of the 1974 World Cup Final programme. Germany certainly found the answer as they defeated the Dutch genius and his team 2–1.

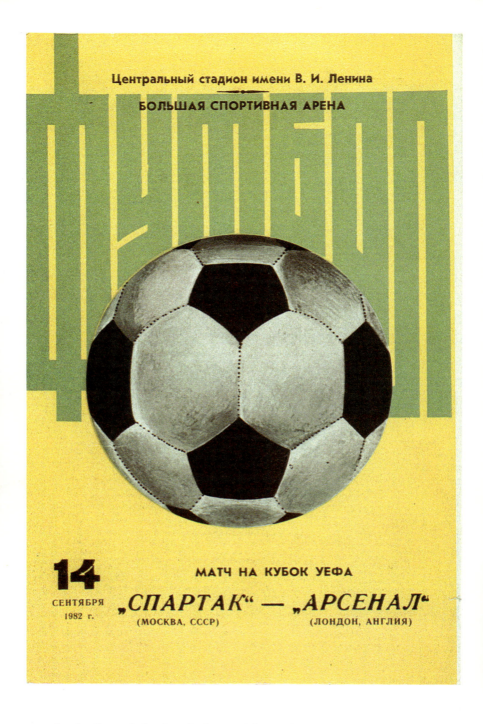

An attractive production from the Russian club Spartak Moscow for the 1982/3 UEFA Cup match with Arsenal.

4.2   A minimum offer published will be set in accordance with market prices previously realised for that or similar items.

5   Factored auctions

5.1   Dealers may auction programmes on behalf of clients. Where these clients have set a minimum offer, it is recommended that they be separately designated to signify that other than the dealer has specified the minimum acceptable offer. Notwithstanding, the item(s) should be auctioned along the normal guidelines.

6   Divulgence of bids

6.1   Dealers may advise those unsuccessful in a bid for a particular item, the realised price of that item, after the expiry date/time — subject to the successful offer being quantifiable in cash terms.

6.2   It is courtesy to reply in the above manner (6.1) where a bidder sends an SAE for this purpose.

6.3   The identity of the successful bidder will not be divulged at any time.

7   Money-back guarantee

7.1   The dealer undertakes to guarantee the return of money (but not necessarily postage expended) where the successful bidder is dissatisfied with the programme, or its condition. Under these circumstances the programme will be re-submitted for auction at a later date, the wording of its description having been reviewed.

Alternative formulae for this procedure, such as listing the previous month's successful bids, or averaging the two highest bids for any item, to allow a more reasonable successful price, are equally open to abuse. The latter would appear to encourage bids of ridiculous proportions, made in the knowledge that the final price would not be nearly so high, unless, of course, two clients both place huge bids and suffer the consequences!

Collector's check list no. 3
Postal auctions/offers supplements

* Decide how much money, in total, you can afford to spend.
* Check your wants list against any offers supplements that you receive.
* Circle or mark the items you require.
* Arrange the desired items in order of most desirable to least desirable.
* Bid against each item in turn, strictly within your financial limitations.
* Place proportionately higher bids against the items you really need.
* Base your bids upon the relative scarcity of items and the expected demand for them, as far as possible.
* Remember that the items you bid for may well appear again soon.
* Don't send your bids in at the last moment or you may miss the deadline. Usually, if bids are equal, it will be the first bid received that secures the item.
* Keep a copy of all offers that you submit.
* Don't bother to ring dealers concerning your bids, offers should be by post only and most dealers will refuse to divulge any information regarding other bids.
* Compare minimum bids between different offers lists to obtain a fairer guide to the price.
* Remember that large postal offers lists will frequently contain items for which no bids will be submitted and which can therefore be obtained at lower prices.
* Smaller offers lists may well be distributed to fewer clients, and chances of success proportionately higher than larger lists.
* The best offers supplements need not be the longest; look for quality rather than quantity.

* Try to avoid bidding for items that are not particularly hard to obtain.
* Offers supplements usually require collectors to remit the total of their successful bids before programmes are sent out, so do ensure that the dealer concerned is reliable.

Other collectors

Collecting hobbies are often lonely ones, but your collection of football programmes can lead to contact with numerous fellow enthusiasts. Happily, communications within the hobby have improved considerably in recent years and there is now ample opportunity to obtain advice, exchange views and news, and to voice opinions on all aspects of collecting.

By meeting and contacting other collectors, or simply reading their views through publications within the hobby, you will soon learn of programmes that you never realised existed, which dealers are the most reliable, and the names of specialists and experts who can help you with your collection. You will also have the opportunity to buy, sell, and exchange items with other collectors, and to share your concerns, give and receive advice, and obtain numerous collecting tips. Collecting should be fun, and sharing the hobby with others can make it all the more enjoyable.

The best ways of staying in touch with other collectors are:

* Subscribe to one or more of the regular publications within the hobby.
* Join a programme club.
* Attend programme fairs; although some fairs can be hectic, you will usually have the opportunity to meet dealers, enthusiasts, and supporters.
* Write a letter to your local football club, asking them to put you in touch with other collectors.
* Enquire at your local supporters' club; if you are a regular supporter, especially at away matches, you will soon encounter other collectors.
* Involve yourself with the hobby, through the pages of its publications, or through the related trade associations and organisations.

Selling your collection

Although the majority of programme collectors aim to collect indefinitely, you may find, for a variety of different reasons, that you wish to sell part, or all, of your collection.

Firstly, you must decide which programmes you wish to sell. Make sure that you really do want to sell them; you may be parting with items that are irreplaceable in some instances. Compile a list of all the items to be sold, carefully noting the condition beside each entry. Always retain a copy of this list. If you wish to sell to a dealer, send your list to several different dealers to obtain the best price. Alternatively, offer your collection to a dealer you know and trust. Large dealers may have the resources to offer higher prices, but do not always do so. It usually pays to shop around. Dealers will often wish to see the collection before they purchase, so ensure that your list, particularly for the condition of items, is accurate. Smaller collections are usually sent by post, and you will either receive a refund of postage costs or have a price quoted that incorporates an element for postage. Ensure that you securely parcel any programmes sent by post, and make full use of the postal services available for sending valuable items. Don't forget to include your name and address, printed clearly, with all correspondence. Most dealers will remit the value of the collection by return of post.

Some dealers also offer to sell clients' programmes on a commission basis, this service usually being available only for old and rare items. Commission rates vary between 10–20%. Although you can obtain higher prices for your rare programmes in this way, remember to allow for the deduction of commission, and remember too, that it takes time to sell them, and that you have no firm guarantee of even doing so.

Purchasing rates can vary considerably between dealers, but on average you can expect one third of the· retail price for your programmes. Common issues will fetch much less than this, but old and rare items will fetch proportionately higher prices. If you sell off only the valuable items, you will usually be left with a large number of worthless programmes. For this reason, it can be better to accept a price for an entire collection rather than selling items individually. Perhaps the most contentious issue between dealers and collectors, is that of purchasing collections. Unfortunately, collectors too often forget that dealers have a living to make, and must, therefore, incorporate an element of profit into their offers to collectors. Whilst you can expect to receive a fair price for programmes you sell, if you are too demanding, or greedy, you will fail to sell any of them.

You may decide to sell your programmes privately. This can be done by advertising through one or more of the magazines published in the hobby, or through the pages of match day programmes. You may already know of other collectors who wish to buy some of your collection. Advertising in your local newspaper can be a good idea to dispose of some of the more common items, especially as many papers provide free advertising for small, private sales. The prices you receive may be higher than those offered by dealers, but it is unlikely that you will find a private collector who wishes to buy all of a large collection. Most private buyers will be searching for individual items from their wants lists.

Many collectors prefer to pass unwanted programmes on to relatives and friends who may be interested in collecting, rather than to sell a collection. Others prefer to keep collecting for as long as possible, sometimes returning with renewed vigour, after several years, to the hobby that they were forced to abandon for various reasons. Many then regret having disposed of parts of their collection, so always be certain that you really do want to sell, before parting with your programmes.

5
The Dealer

dealer (ˈdiːlə) *n*. a person or firm engaged
in commercial purchase and sale.

The Market

The size of the market available to dealers operating within the hobby of programme collecting today is somewhat debatable. Estimates of the total market fluctuate wildly between 2,000 and 20,000 or more collectors. What there can be no doubting, however, is the fact that it is an extremely competitive market, with a large number of dealers competing for a limited amount of trade. Many of these dealers are small, part-time operators, although an established network of full-time dealers has been in operation for many years. Part-time dealers (or 'traders', as they are usually called by full-time dealers) have the advantage of alternative sources of income, and do not rely entirely upon the hobby for a living. Much to the chagrin of full-time businesses, the part-time operator can make a sizeable amount of 'pocket money', usually tax free, from occasional appearances at trade fairs and irregular issues of catalogues or lists.

There are few opportunities, however, to make easy money in this business environment. Many newcomers to the trade are loathed to commit themselves full-time to a market that has been largely cornered by a few established dealers. Certainly, a considerable amount of capital would be required to compete with these larger dealers, who have worked hard to build their businesses over a period of years, having adopted efficient and often vigorous marketing techniques to safeguard their livelihoods. These dealers are further protected by a high degree of customer loyalty within the hobby. Indeed, some dealers appear to rely almost solely upon the protection afforded by customer loyalty and geographical spread, whilst others attempt to avoid intense competition by specialising in certain clubs or collecting categories.

There has been a slow, but inevitable, decline in the number of dealers entering the hobby in recent years, either through seeing the market as having reached saturation point, or through a general reluctance to enter a trade that has possibly peaked already. The football programme market often follows the rather unstable fortunes of its parent sport with unerring accuracy, and is always prone to the eccentricities of collectors and to the dynamic market forces of supply and demand.

The market has certainly experienced a large degree of consolidation over the past few years, with fewer collectors now entering the hobby, but with existing enthusiasts entering into more transactions than before with dealers, as they pursue wanted items with relish. Club shops, so often the only source of some programmes for collectors in the past, have suffered through the increased market dominance by dealers. Without the guidance of a national programme club, the volume of trade, correspondence, and exchanges, between fellow collectors also appears to have fallen considerably. In recent years, almost inevitably, the hobby has developed an increasingly commercial attitude.

The market has been flooded with common league issues for the past fifteen to twenty seasons, and many dealers have been left with a large quantity of almost valueless stock. The trade in rare programmes, mainly through the increased use of offers supplements, has taken on a new lease of life, and prices of such items continue to soar. Dealers have been an obvious target for abuse as prices of programmes in general continue to rise, but clubs have been quick to recognise the increased commercial potential of match day publications, and collectors themselves have been guilty through their undisguised and often frenzied enthusiasm to obtain desired items at any cost. The majority of dealers are hardworking, knowledgeable, and reliable, but have suffered some bad press due to the misconduct of a small minority (a trait all too familiar in the sport of football). The market has also experienced continued resistance by many dealers against attempts to present a more acceptable and professional face of programme collecting to the world at large, through the development and consolidation of trade associations.

Starting up

Converting a hobby into a business is always a difficult task. The motivation behind a hobby is pleasure; the motivation behind a business is invariably profit. These differing objectives can cause conflict, which is probably why most aspiring dealers start on a part-time basis. To start a full-time business also requires a substantial sum of capital, which is soon tied up in stock for lengthy periods. Few small businesses make a profit in their first six months of trading, and many potential newcomers to the programme trade fall by the wayside during this difficult period. Usually, the initial causes of failure are: lack of organisation, insufficient capital, shortage of stock, or over-stocking with slow moving stock (which can cause severe cashflow problems). In addition, some new traders have an inadequate amount of time available to devote to their new business, even on a part-time basis, which results in rapid evaporation of enthusiasm and subsequent failure.

The football programme market, unlike some collecting hobbies, operates in a volatile, high-risk environment that follows the fluctuating fortunes of our national game. A great deal of dedication, application, and many hours of hard work, are required if you are to succeed in such a competitive market. You will need to plan carefully, invest sensibly, and organise efficiently. A professional attitude is required at all times, no matter what scale you are operating on. Reputation counts for a great deal in collecting circles, and it is essential to establish yourself as a reliable and honest dealer.

Although selling programmes can attract a number of enthusiasts on the look out for a quick profit, entry into the market usually signifies a long-term commitment. In general, dealers make only a moderate return on their money invested and in relation to effort expended. If one were to calculate an hourly rate for programme dealers, it would probably be enough to discourage all but the boldest from entering the trade! For many, it is almost a labour of love, with only a small amount of profit, but a large amount of enjoyment and satisfaction to be derived from the business. Interest in the sport of football is a prerequisite for operating a programme business.

Dealers almost invariably start dealing on a part-time basis, and many never make the transition to a full-time business. The business usually starts with programmes that have been stock-piled over a period of months, or even years. These form the basis of the dealer's opening stock, with the rest being obtained via a concerted advertising and purchasing campaign shortly before producing the first catalogue or lists. Some traders prefer to start by taking their limited stocks to programme fairs, and ploughing back any profits made at these events into their businesses.

Choosing the correct business form is of the utmost importance. Many dealers start as, and remain as, sole traders. Although in this situation, the risk is carried by the individual alone, the initial volume of trade is unlikely to justify the inclusion of more than one person in the concern, and ultimately the sole trader will reap all the rewards that accrue to the business. Others find the attraction of having someone to share the costs, and help with the running of the business, a lure that is impossible to refuse. An additional person to share the responsibilities, however, is also an extra person to share the profits, and unless the business is extremely lucrative and successful, there will be few profits for either partner. All too often, partnership agreements, whether formal or informal, are entered into by the unlikeliest of trading partners and, inevitably, these ill-conceived arrangements end in disaster.

It is extremely unlikely that any trader will ever need to operate as a limited company; the mass of paperwork and formalities associated with this business form alone are enough to discourage most.

Most dealers trade under their individual names, although some prefer to select an appropriate business name. The law regarding registration of business names has changed in recent years, and at present the only requirement for sole traders, is that the proprietor's name and business address should appear on official stationery.

Getting the paperwork right is essential for any business. Too many traders fail to properly establish and maintain accurate books and records. This blunts the efficiency of their business and prevents them from being as successful as they could be. It can also cause problems if they are required to submit tax returns. It is very important for you to cultivate a competent and professional image. Business stationery is a part of this overall public image, and having compliment slips, order forms, and letter headings professionally printed should be quite inexpensive. A set of accounts books, index cards (for customer files and for mailing lists), and a postage book will also be required. A bank account should be opened separately for the business, and your appropriate requirements discussed with your bank manager. You should discuss with him the costs involved, your expected cashflow, and the availability of overdraft arrangements, should you require them. The Inland Revenue, and Department of Health and Social Security, will also need to be notified, for tax and national insurance reasons.

Many part-time traders operate their businesses from home. This has the advantage of keeping overheads, such as light, heat, power and telephone costs, to a minimum. It also removes the need to find business premises, and the associated costs of rent and rates. You could find that planning permission is required, however, before the local authority will allow a business to be run from home. Alternatively, correspondence addresses, or Post Office Boxes, are quite inexpensive to rent and can be convenient.

Wherever the business is operated from, there must be adequate and appropriate storage space, as football programmes are rather bulky. It is also strongly recommended that ground floor storage facilities are found; ceiling repairs can be rather expensive! Moving boxes of stock up and down flights of stairs can also be exhausting, and a strong deterrent against attending too many programme fairs (when a large proportion of your stock will need to be moved). Programmes must be stored in strong containers, boxes, or binders, as appropriate, and a number of sturdy shelf units will be needed.

Your football programme business will only be as strong as the quality and quantity of your stock, and the size of your mailing list. Different sources of stock are discussed later in this chapter, but it is important not to invest too much capital in cheaper, slow-moving stock. Although a larger number of such programmes can be bought, they will take several months to sell; in the meantime your creditors will need to be paid. There will also be insufficient cash available for you to purchase good stock, should the opportunity arise. Cashflow problems usually arise in this way, and can cause the premature demise of even the largest concern. It is a good idea to plan income and expenditure over a period of time, to reduce the chances of this problem occurring.

You will need to assess the competition that you are likely to face when you first enter the market. If there are already several dealers operating in your locality, you may have to specialise in certain clubs, or collecting categories, in order to survive. If you set out to provide exactly the same service that these existing dealers already provide, it is unlikely that you will meet with much success.

Specialisation has the advantage of allowing you to corner a section of the market for yourself. You will also find that it is easy to build up a detailed knowledge of the programmes that you stock, in only a short space of time. This will enable you to provide a better service to your customers, and ensure that you obtain the best possible prices for individual items. Your mailing list will soon consist of a select, loyal, band of customers who specialise in the collecting categories that you stock. Your basic stock will remain quite stable, which should make the compilation of lists and catalogues an easier task. There are disadvantages, however, with specialisation, which many disregard for being a 'putting all your eggs in one basket' policy. Your catalogues may look rather similar, issue after

94

issue, which can act as a disincentive for collectors to buy. The general collector is not likely to be very interested in your lists either, especially with so many other dealers to choose from. If you only specialise in a particular club, it can be a very dangerous policy, as your business fortunes will usually follow the footballing fortunes of that club. Good news of course, if you had chosen to specialise in Wimbledon programmes back in the 1960's! The other main problem with specialisation, is obtaining stock. You will have a continuous turnover of some items of stock, and will always be searching for rare and interesting programmes to replace them, if your stock is to avoid stagnation.

Many businesses fail to establish themselves simply because collectors are not aware that they even exist! You will need to advertise your business enthusiastically in the first few months of trading, through the numerous magazines and advertising supplements that circulate in the hobby. Most of these publications offer discounts for block bookings, and advertising rates in general within the hobby are quite inexpensive.

In the collecting market, entry is often easier than exit. Selling programmes at retail prices will yield a modest profit, but closing a business usually means disposing of the bulk of your stock at wholesale prices, or even at cost. Many a dealer has discovered his exit from the hobby blocked by this discrepancy between retail and realisable values of stock. Even so, establishing yourself in the football programme collecting market, with its vast range of stock, and its often charismatic clientele, can be a challenging, fascinating, and enjoyable experience.

Catalogues and Mailing Lists

As the bulk of football programme business is conducted by mail order, the presentation and content of the dealer's catalogue, or lists, is of primary importance. The content should be easily read, divided into appropriate sections, correctly priced, and have the condition of items clearly described (using standard abbreviations, as shown below). The presentation should be both attractive and professional, as the catalogue is the first (and sometimes, only) part of your business that the potential customer will see.

You should send for other dealers' catalogues, to acquaint yourself with their prices, abbreviations, and format used. Try to look at ways of improving the presentation. If you were given the catalogue, would you be able to locate the programmes you wanted? Would you want to order from the catalogue?

Many catalogues and lists are now stored in word processors and computers, which can save hours of work previously spent hunched over a typewriter! Ask any dealer which part of his business he dislikes the most, and he will almost certainly reply, 'preparing my catalogue'. First, there is the stock-take, which will almost certainly be manual, as very few businesses are able to fully computerise stock as diverse as football programmes. This involves checking almost every item in stock against the previous list or catalogue, and noting deletions from, and additions to, stock. Recording the condition of individual items will also be necessary. If you are preparing your very first catalogue, this task will be even more arduous. Even computerised stock systems are time-consuming, as full records of programmes bought and sold, and their condition, will still need to be entered into the computer.

Having listed amendments to stock, you will now need to

price items. You will almost certainly have to refer to other dealers' catalogues to discover the prices of some programmes. Others you may have to make calculated guesses for, based upon market prices in general, and how much you paid for the items in the first place. Note the price beside individual items on your stock list as required. Many programmes can be listed and priced by seasons, but there are always rare and sought-after items within a particular season. Prices do fluctuate between dealers, but if your prices are wildly different, you will probably lose trade.

Standard abbreviations used in dealers' catalogues include: cr − creased; slcr − slight crease; vslcr − very slight crease; rs − rusty staples; cell − cellotaped; tc − team changes entered; sof − score on face; nof − number on face; wof − writing on face; gr − grubby; mk − marked; fld − folded; ph − punched holes; vgc − very good condition; tm − token missing; ss − single sheet.

Printing costs can vary considerably, and it definitely pays to shop around for the best price. Some printers will require you to submit finished proofs of your catalogue, which will mean you typing pages out individually, unless you have access to a word processor. Other printers will offer you their own word processing facilities at a set hourly rate, which can prove to be good value for money. In this case, after the initial setting up costs, you will supply amendments to previous catalogues, and only pay for the time involved in entering these alterations, and for the final printing costs. You will usually have to provide any finished artwork (such as the cover design) yourself. Remember to give the printers plenty of time to prepare your lists, although most will be able to complete your order within a week.

Some dealers prefer to produce individual club lists, which are then sent out on request, rather than issuing regular catalogues. This has the advantage of cutting down on printing costs and time-consuming preparation, but can restrict sales, as collectors will not be able to see the full range of stock that is available for sale.

Although most catalogues are issued free of charge, it is

usual to make a small charge to cover postage costs. It is a good idea to offer discounts on an annual subscription, as many collectors will forget to send for your catalogues each time they are produced. You will then only have to remind customers that their subscription is due for renewal each year.

Always include an order form with your catalogues, preferably loose, so that the collector does not have to tear the catalogue to remove it. The order form should be set out to include columns for the page number, season, description of item, condition, and price. Remember to include postage details on the form; you may be surprised at first to see just how heavy a few football programmes can be. It is a good idea to send orders over a certain amount post-free. This is the equivalent of offering a discount on larger orders, and can act as an incentive for collectors to buy more programmes, thus avoiding the costly element of postage.

When studying individual dealers' lists, collectors will look for a good variety of programmes (even within a specific collecting category), the number of rare items listed (separate from offers list items), quality (including, therefore, accuracy of description), and price. They will also study the image, presentation, layout, and clarity of your catalogue, as well as noting the consistency of its issue and its cost.

Ensure that orders are despatched promptly, and always try to take the time to reply to collectors' letters and queries. Faulty stock should always be guaranteed, and replaced within a certain time limit, or a full refund offered. Package orders securely in padded envelopes, or backed with cardboard, and send expensive items by the appropriate postal service (recorded post, or parcel insurance service, for example). If you pay attention to small details such as these, and prepare your first catalogue carefully, you should be receiving numerous orders within a short space of time, providing you have established a good-sized mailing list.

Obtaining a mailing list is certainly not as difficult as it may first appear, although it can prove to be a rather lengthy process. You will find the names and addresses of many collectors in the pages of trade magazines and publications, particularly in the classified advertising sections. There are also a number of advertising supplements in circulation within the hobby, and more customers can be located in this way. Through your own advertising, you will receive numerous enquiries, and should note the relevant customer details on your record cards, as you obtain them. These customer record cards will form much more than merely a mailing list, and details of subscriptions paid, orders received and sent, and collecting interests, should all be noted. You will find that within a few months, your mailing list will have grown rapidly. Your business should then continue to expand steadily, in line with the growing number of collectors on your books.

Sources of stock

Most dealers would agree that selling good stock is easy. However, obtaining good stock can sometimes be far from easy, and if the continued demands of the collector are not met, then the dealer will soon experience a significant loss in trade.

It is important to remain fair and consistent with your buying prices for programmes. Your reputation as an honest and reliable dealer will never be more at risk than during negotiations for purchasing collections. Most large collections will contain items that are quite rare, amongst a hoard of items that are almost valueless. Generally, this means that you will have to average out your offer for the better items, to compensate for the less desirable majority. You will frequently be asked to value collections, by people who clearly have no intention of selling them. Some dealers refuse to spend time on a valuation for programmes, unless they know that they have a chance of purchasing them. Others are only too pleased to allow the public the benefit of their knowledge and experience. You will undoubtedly decide for yourself which policy you wish to pursue.

The best sources of stock include:

* Advertising through various media:
  National newspapers.
  Local newspapers.
  Football club programmes.
  Specialist magazines (*Exchange & Mart*, for example).
  Trade magazines.
  Advertising circulars/supplements within the hobby.
  Postcard advertisements in local Post Offices and newsagents.
* Antiques/collectors/ephemera fairs.

* Second-hand/antique/house-clearance shops and businesses.
* Book dealers and shops.
* Car-boot sales/fetes/bazaars.
* Classified Ads of local newspapers.
* Collectors.
* Personal contacts.
* Football clubs.
* Match day programme printers.
* Wholesale dealers.
* Other dealers (often on an exchange basis).

If you have to travel to look at a collection, make an allowance for time and mileage costs in your assessment of the value of the items. If you decide not to view the items, be careful not to commit yourself to a definite price until you have had a chance to verify the condition and validity of the programmes that have been offered to you. If people wish to send programmes through the post to you, always advise them to package the items securely. Allow for these postage costs in your valuation of the collection.

Above all, never buy programmes that you cannot sell. Too many dealers waste considerable sums of money by purchasing stock that is not only slow-moving, but in many cases, is unlikely to sell at all.

Programme Fairs

A great deal of time in the hobby is devoted to the often controversial subject of programme fairs. These events are of considerable importance to dealers, particularly full-time operators, and represent much more than just an opportunity to make a quick profit. The element of public relations, and the importance of fairs in the development of the hobby, cannot be over-emphasised. The need to encourage newcomers, and younger collectors in particular, is all too evident in the hobby today. Programme fairs provide an ideal opportunity to portray the hobby in a favourable light to these potential enthusiasts.

Fairs remain objects of fascination to the public, but appear to defy all known commercial rules; predicting an attendance for even the best-organised fair is about as easy as nominating the winner of the Grand National! A well-publicised, efficiently organised big city fair may only attract 100 enthusiasts; a small town fair, held at a Fourth Division Club ground, may draw as many as 250 visitors. Falling attendances may be the result of too many of these events saturating a limited market (for most, the novelty value of programme fairs having been lost long ago), or represent a failure, through poor marketing and organisation, to fully realise the potential of such occasions.

Too many people seem to regard programme fairs from a purely commercial viewpoint, hoping for a good return from a day's trading, and seeking an opportunity to dispose of some of the slower-moving items of stock. Too few seek to provide the necessary entertainment, interest, and comfort, sought by the collector. All too often, these events can degenerate into an unruly scrum for bargains. Fairs do need to be carefully organised, substantially advertised, and have a number of renowned dealers in attendance. Exhibitions, displays, and the provision of refreshments, in a relaxed and informal atmosphere, will make the day successful and enjoyable for all.

Programme fairs are, in reality, large public relations exercises, where goods and services are exhibited, introductions are made, and future trade is initiated. Investment, in terms of marketing and public relations, can reap far more future benefits than a large cash profit at the end of the day's trading. Providing the dealer can cover his expenses, and hopefully show a small working profit, he should be measuring the success of the event by the number of programmes purchased, and by the numerous new contacts and customers obtained during the day.

Preparation for Programme Fairs

Just as it is important for fairs to be efficiently organised, so it is important for the dealers attending these events to be well prepared. A successful day is not entirely dependent upon the organisers. Ensuring that your stall will be in some semblance of order on the day, and that the quality and quantity of stock is suitable for the occasion, is equally important.

Before committing yourself to attending an event, you should check that the location is suitable, which other dealers will be in attendance, and whether the fair is being adequately publicised. If attending the fair involves a long journey, remember to include the time and mileage involved in your costs for the day. Ensure that you have suitable transport for moving a large number of football programmes.

When studying the location, check the availability of nearby parking facilities, and access to the premises for loading and unloading. You should also be familiar with the stall sizes and layout, and whether display boards or pin boards will be supplied for your use. The overall environment and facilities available, and the prospective trade facing you on the day, will strongly influence your plans for the event. You will then be able to judge for yourself whether the cost of a stall at the fair is reasonable.

Choosing the appropriate stock for a programme fair can be a very difficult task, mainly because predicting expected demand for specific programmes is almost impossible. Logically, if you were attending a trade fair in Manchester, you would expect to sell more Manchester club programmes than any others. However, you are equally likely to find enthusiastic collectors seeking Birmingham, Ipswich or Scunthorpe programmes! It is therefore important that you take a good variety of stock with you, but with the emphasis upon clubs within the region immediately surrounding the programme fair location.

There were days when many dealers used to take mainly slow-moving stock to programme fairs. In today's competitive market, it is wiser to take a selection of programmes that includes a larger proportion of rarer, more saleable issues. Take care that you do not damage stock in transit; programmes should be carefully stored in sturdy boxes (there are many suitable custom-built plastic containers on the market), with rare items transported in separate binders or folders. Carefully sort and label stock, and price as many items as possible — it saves time, and collectors are often encouraged to buy if they can see a definite price for a desired programme.

Most of your takings on the day will be in cash, so it is wise to take a secure cash tin. An adequate cash float will also be required to start the day, or you may find yourself short of change. You may also need your cheque book if you are offered any rare items at the fair. A pen and paper, together with a few cards or labels, are useful for noting down names and addresses of contacts and new customers. A supply of promotional material, and copies of your latest lists or catalogue, will provide useful advertising for your business, as well as showing the public what your full range of stock includes. It is a good idea to plan a small display for the event, which can include some of the rarer programmes that you have in stock. You will find that by displaying such signs as 'If you can't find the items you want, please ask' and 'Collections purchased, best cash prices offered', the more reticent visitors to the event will be encouraged to approach your stall.

Finally, attending programme fairs does involve hard work and can be quite tiring, and it is unlikely that you will be able to survive the day without a reliable friend or assistant to help you! If you plan carefully, well in advance of the event, then your day at the programme fair should be both satisfying and successful.

Organising Programme Fairs

Of the many programme fairs that are organised each year within the hobby, a large number fail to be as successful as they could be, due primarily to poor planning, insufficient publicity, and inefficient organisation. By attending to a few basic requirements, organising these events can be both simple and satisfying:

* PLAN carefully, and well in advance.
* PUBLICISE effectively through local media, widely through publications within the hobby, and also through the pages of various club programmes.
* TIME the fair to coincide with other complementary events (such as a fair in the morning, and a football match in the afternoon). Don't clash with other events. Don't start too early or finish too late.
* LOCATION of the fair should be easily accessible, with parking facilities nearby.
* ACCESS to the premises should be early enough to allow dealers plenty of time to set up before the fair commences.
* LAYOUT should be spacious, adequate for the number of dealers, and safe. Check fire regulations and maximum numbers allowed.
* STALLS must be well spaced, and large enough to meet the needs of all dealers. Don't forget to provide chairs.
* STAFFING should include a doorman and enquiries assistant as minimum.
* FACILITIES will usually include bar and refreshments, toilets, display boards, and adequate numbers of tables and chairs.
* INTEREST in the event can be enhanced by use of displays, exhibitions, football videos, and competitions. Provide an admission programme whenever possible.
* COSTS of stalls, and admission revenue, should be adequate

to cover organising costs such as hall hire, staffing, publicity, and miscellaneous expenses.

Careful planning and preparation is time well spent, and will mean less work on the actual day. Publicity is probably the most important aspect, but it is pointless having hundreds of enthusiastic collectors attending a poorly organised fair; it will certainly put them off visiting the next one!

The aim of organising a programme fair is, primarily, to provide publicity for the hobby of football programme collecting, and to provide a means for collectors and dealers to meet, and trade, to their mutual benefit. It should be quite possible to organise a programme fair so that all costs are covered, and so that all those involved with the event can enjoy an interesting, enjoyable, and well-spent day.

Mail order tips

The vast majority of all trade in the hobby of football programme collecting, is conducted by mail order. You will soon
establish your own system for marketing your business, and
dealing with orders and enquiries, but you may find the following tips useful:

* Most mail order buyers purchase by post because the
  dealer can offer goods or services that are unobtainable
  locally.
* The success of your business will depend upon:
  The items that you have available for sale.
  The service that you can offer your customers.
  Your ability to organise your business.
  The way you choose to expand your trade.
* Create yourself a professional and reliable image.
* Establish and maintain basic records and files, including:
  Advertising files.
  Supplier/purchase files.
  Financial files and accounts.
  Customer orders.
  Correspondence files.
  Competitor files.
* Research your prospective market to determine competition,
  advertising outlets, and budget requirements.
* Select your market.
* Cultivate sources of stock.
* Price stock according to market prices, and how much it cost
  you.
* Advertisements are your investment in the future of your
  business:
  Classified advertisements are usually inexpensive and cost-
  effective.

Display advertisements convey an image of a larger scale business, and can draw a better response.
* When selecting publications to advertise in, consider the costs, related to the prospective market size.
* Maintain records of your advertising; the costs, the response, and the cost-effectiveness, of each advert.
* Fulfil orders quickly and accurately, especially to new customers.
* Package items securely, to avoid damage in transit.
* Answer enquiries quickly and politely.
* Avoid over-stocking.
* Try to clear unprofitable, slow-moving stock.
* Make good use of discounts, special offers, and sale items.
* Keep strict and accurate records.
* Separate your money from business money.
* Retain some of your profits in the business.

If you do decide to start dealing in football programmes, you will need time to establish your business. You will also need a strong interest in the game of football, and a dedication to the hobby. Providing you plan ahead, and organise your business efficiently, you should find the football programme market both fascinating and rewarding.

Trading Places

In any trading relationship, there are always problems that will be encountered, and the dealer and the collector in the football programme market soon discover that they are no exception to this rule. The majority of problems are caused by simple misunderstandings, misconceptions, or through a basic failure to appreciate an alternative viewpoint.

For many collectors, the first (and sometimes, only) contact with dealers, is through the post. With no guarantee that the dealer they have contacted is either reliable or honest, this results at first in a natural degree of suspicion and reservation. They must then cope with some inevitable delays in receiving replies to correspondence and orders, accept refusals by some dealers to even acknowledge enquiries, and deal with faulty goods when received. They are also faced with rising prices, and an increasingly commercial attitude by many within the hobby.

Meanwhile, the dealer is faced with a deluge of anonymous orders and enquiries, from enthusiasts who were in such a hurry to post their correspondence, that they forgot to include their names and addresses. There is the problem of the indecipherable, often illegible, scribble that passes for handwriting, and also the number of insufficient remittances that are so often enclosed with orders. Then there are the inevitable lists of programmes sent for valuation (which will, in all probability, be used by the enquirer as a base figure for future negotiations elsewhere), and wants lists that run to hundreds of items. Faced with falling demand in some areas of collecting, but with a steady flow of incoming bills to be met, it is hardly surprising that fewer dealers are now entering the hobby.

Ask any dealer to recommend a few guidelines for collectors, and he will probably include the following:

110

* Always include your name and address in all correspondence.
* Print all details clearly.
* Remember to notify all changes of address as soon as possible.
* Always include an SAE, or stamps, if you wish for a reply.
* Ensure that you send sufficient remittance to cover the cost of enquiries and orders.
* Keep wants lists to a minimum.
* Accept that receiving occasional damaged items is inevitable. Return them promptly, with a request for refund or replacement.
* Don't expect to receive too much for programmes that you sell back to dealers.
* Remember that dealers do have a living to make, and that most receive only a moderate return from sales.

Similar guidelines for dealers would probably then be offered by collectors:

* It is courtesy to reply to enquiries, especially if an SAE is enclosed.
* Issue cash refunds for faulty or out of stock items wherever possible.
* Send out orders promptly.
* Package all orders securely.
* Describe the condition of items carefully, and accurately, in lists and catalogues.
* Ensure that the programmes you send out are actually the ones that were ordered.
* If you must use offers supplements, only use them for very rare items.
* Always offer fair prices for purchasing collections.
* Include your name, address, and, if applicable, telephone number, on correspondence and in advertisements.
* Try to be helpful to collectors, and polite in answering queries.

If both parties involved in football programme trade made an effort to follow these guidelines, there would undoubtedly be fewer disputes within the hobby. Unfortunately, too many dealers and collectors suffer from the same major blind spot — they both think that they are right!

6
Dealer Directory

Dealer Details

Key: prop. − Proprietor or owner; Pt − Part-time; Ft − Full-time; E − date business established; Stk − range of programmes stocked; Cat − Catalogue or lists issued; N − Number of issues per year; C − cost per issue; S − Annual subscription cost; OS − offers supplement inclusive; OS/S − offers supplement separate; TO − telephone orders accepted (9am to 5pm unless otherwise stated); WL − Wants list service offered; PACT − PACT member.

AIS programmes. prop. Brian James, 5 South Square, Boston, Lincs PE21 6JA. Tel. 0205-311333. Pt. E1984. Stk: General. Cat. N8. C25p. TO. WL.

Brentside Programmes. prop. Chris Ward, 19 Fishers Mead, Puckeridge, Herts SG11 1SP. Tel. 0920-822720. Ft. E1978. Stk: Wide range pre-war to date. Cat. N8. C30p. OS. TO 9.30am to 9pm. PACT.

Channel Programmes. prop. J. D. Whelan and T. A. Lomax, White Lodge, Bruce Lane, St Peter Port, Guernsey, Channel Islands. Tel. 0481-23157. Ft. E1985. Stk: English league 1950's to date, Scottish, Non-league and Big Match. Cat. N4. C30p. TO.

Steve Earl Football Programmes. prop. Steve Earl, St Mary's Parish Rooms, Broad Street, Bungay, Suffolk NR35 1AH. Tel. 0986-2621 or 0986-4108. Ft. E1970. Stk: Mint Condition Big Match and General League. Cat. N1. C-Free, with occasional supplement.

Football Crazy. prop. Alan Cunningham, 13A Spittal Street, Edinburgh EH3 9DY. Tel. 031-228-2633. Ft. E1981. Stk: General, Scottish & Irish specialist. Cat. N12. C25p. S £2.80. OS. TO. WL.

Peter Holtom Programmes. prop. Peter Holtom, PO Box 2, Harold Wood, Romford, Essex RM3 0PA. Tel. 04023-73469. Ft. E1975. Stk: Current season. Cat. N10. C20p. TO. WL. PACT.

Leeds United AFC Programme Cabin. prop. Leeds United AFC, Elland Road, Leeds LS11 0ES. Tel. Leeds 706844. Ft. Stk: Leeds United, Internationals, Cup Finals, General league. Cat. N2. WL — send SAE.

Portman Programmes. prop. Julian Earwaker, 18 Lower Brook Street, Ipswich, Suffolk IP4 1AL. Tel. 0473-56447. Pt. E1983. Stk: Wide range pre-war to date, Ipswich Town specialist. Cat. N5. C25p. S £1. OS.

Programme Promotions. prop. David Allen, 14 Wheatlands, Heston, Hounslow, Middlesex TW5 0SA. Tel. 01-570-7458. Ft. E1986. Stk: Wide range pre-war to date. Cat. N6. C30p. OS. TO 8.30am to 10.30pm. WL. PACT.

Dick Rattray Football Programmes. prop. Dick Rattray, 6 The Sycamores, Boxmoor, Hemel Hempstead, Herts HP3 0LL. Tel. 0442-64210. Ft. E1978. Stk: Wide range. Cat. N10. C — postage only. OS. TO. PACT.

Scandinavian Programme Club. prop. Stig Forsingdal, 4–6 Av. Victor Hugo, L-1750, Luxembourg. Tel. Luxembourg 462348. Pt. E1972. Stk: European programmes, Statistical annuals, lapel badges. Cat. N1. C £1.

Slough Town Supporters Association Club Shop, c/o Kingsway, Church Street, Slough, Berks SL1 1SZ. Tel. Slough 823822. Pt. E1984. Stk: General league, Non-league, Big Match & souvenirs. Cat. N4. C30p + SAE. OS (alternate issues). TO 7.30pm to 9.30pm. WL.

Southern-progs, 38 Tithe Walk, Mill Hill, London NW7 2QA. Pt. E1976. Stk: Wide range pre-war to date, Arsenal, Chelsea, Tottenham special sections. Cat. N4. C25p. PACT.

Sports Programmes. prop. Tony Stanford and Roy Calmels, PO Box 74, Chapel Street, Coventry CV1 4AB. Tel. 0203-28672. Ft. E1973. Stk: All categories, Britain's largest antique programme dealers. Cat. N8, Non-league Cat. N6, Postal Auction Cat. N6. C35p. OS/S. TO. PACT.

David Stacey Publications. prop. David Stacey, 66 Southend Road, Wickford, Essex SS11 8EN. Tel. 0268-732041. Ft. Stk: Current league, Big Match, Specials, Bundles. Cat. N12. C – free. PACT.

Stevens Programmes. prop. Phil Stevens, 108 Wordsworth Drive, Taunton, Somerset TA1 2HL. Pt. E1983. Stk: Post-1970 General league and cup. Cat. N4. C30p. OS. TO 9am to 5pm Taunton 252945, 6pm to 10pm Taunton 277080. WL.

Sunnymeade (Oxford) Programmes. prop. Graham Cook, 6 Harpes Road, Summertown, Oxford OX2 7QL. Tel. 0865-52726. Pt. E1982. Stk: Oxford United specialist. Cat. N2. C40p. TO. WL.

Julian Taylor Programmes. prop. Julian Taylor, 32 Lower Howsel Road, Malvern Link, Worcs WR14 1ED. Tel. 06845-4845. Ft. E1979. Stk: Wide range. Cat. General, Non-league, or Individual lists. N6. C – free. TO. WL.

DC Young Programmes. prop. David Young, 8 Birkdale Mount, Leeds LS17 7SS. Tel. 0532-694537. Pt. Stk: General, 1940's to date, Leeds United special section. Cat. N2. TO weekdays 6.15pm to 9.30pm, weekends 10am to 9pm. WL.

LIST OF MEMBERS

ROY CALMELS & TONY STANFORD T/A Sports Programme, P.O. Box 74, Chapel St, Coventry, CV1 4AB.

JOHN WILSON P.O. Box 61, York, YO1 1FG.

DICK RATTRAY 6, The Sycamores, Boxmoor, Hemel Hempstead, Herts, HP3 0LL.

SOUTHERN PROGRAMMES 38, Tithe Walk, Mill Hill, London, NW7 2QA.

DAVID STACEY PUBLICATIONS 66, Southend Road, Wickford, Essex, SS11 8EN.

PETER HOLTOM 22, Tindall Close, Romford, Essex, RM3 0PA.

MARTIN SILVERMAN 9, Home Mead, Stanmore, Middx, HA7 1AF.

RICHARD COHEN 6, Handel Close, Edgware, Middx.

BARRY SWASH T/A South Staffs Programmes, 16, Mellish Road, Walsall, West Midlands, WS4 2ED.

ELLIS SCHWARTZ 4, Millhaven Close, Chadwell Heath, Romford, Essex, RM6 4PL.

JOHN GARRARD T/A Midland Programme Shop, 253, Oxhill Road, Handsworth, Birmingham.

BARRY ELLISON T/A Chorley Programmes, 51 Park Ave., Euxton, Chorley, Lancs, PR7 6JQ.

GEORGE WILLIAMS 8, Edward Close, St Albans, Herts, AL1 5EN.

KATH & PETER RUNDO 4, Crawford Ave., Gauldry, Newport-on-Tay, Scotland, DD6 8SG. 082–624–356.

PETER RICHES 5, Station Parade, Dorchester Road, Northolt Park, Middx.

CHRIS WARD T/A Brentside Programmes, 19, Fishers Mead, Puckeridge, Herts, SG11 1SP.

COLIN BOULTER 2, Greenhill Drive, Barwell, Leics, LE9 8BW.

DAVID ALLEN T/A/ Programme Promotions, 14, Wheatlands, Heston, Hounslow, Middx, TW5 0SA.

LEN LLEWELLYN 45, Millfield, High Ongar, Essex, CM5 9RJ.

Correct at 1/3/87

The following are office bearers on the committee.
ROY CALMELS (Chairman)
JOHN WILSON (Vice Chairman)
DICK RATTRAY (Secretary)

THE INDEPENDENT TRADE ASSOCIATION FOR THE HOBBY OF
FOOTBALL PROGRAMME COLLECTING

7
Gallery

Gallery

A collection of football programmes provides a visual feast that will appeal to enthusiasts of all ages. Throughout the years a vast range of publications have been produced, providing an enormous variety of covers, cartoons, photographs, and advertisements.

Whether your interest in football programmes is fuelled by historical curiosity, a passion for the sport of soccer, nostalgia, or pure inquisitiveness, you will surely find the contents of such publications both absorbing and enjoyable.

A lovely example of the changing face of soccer. What would today's players think of the famous 'Mansfield-Hotspurs' football boot?

THE FOOTBALL ASSOCIATION CHALLENGE CUP COMPETITION

FINAL TIE

BLACKPOOL v BOLTON WANDERERS

SATURDAY, MAY 2nd, 1953   KICK-OFF 3 pm

EMPIRE STADIUM

WEMBLEY

Chairman and Managing Director :   SIR ARTHUR J. ELVIN, M.B.E.

OFFICIAL PROGRAMME · ONE SHILLING

A winner's medal at last for the great Stanley Matthews as his Blackpool team defeat Nat Lofthouse and his Bolton colleagues 4–3 in the 1953 FA Cup Final at Wembley.

ACCRINGTON STANLEY F.C.

(1921) LTD.

PEEL PARK GROUND, ACCRINGTON

OFFICIAL PROGRAMME - THREEPENCE

AFTER THE MATCH—

SNACKS - DRINKS *(Hot and Cold)*
and a
VARIETY OF SANDWICHES

SNACK **Melbo** BAR

(Opposite Manchester Bus Stop)
MELBOURNE STREET, ACCRINGTON
Quick Service — 7 days a week — Open till 10 p.m.

Tel. 2496   Tel. 2496

RAILWAY HOTEL
(RESIDENTIAL)

BLACKBURN ROAD, ACCRINGTON

*Thwaites Ales served under the most
hygienic conditions.* Wines & Spirits

Printed by Shuttleworths (Printers) Ltd., Wellington Press, Accrington.

*Accrington Stanley were once a force to be reckoned with in British soccer, but then retired from
the Football League during the 1961/2 season. This programme is from the 1959/60 season.*

ALLIED
INTERNATIONAL

ARSENAL

v.

SPARTA

AT

HIGHBURY

Wednesday, October 2nd, 1946

KICK OFF 3.30 P.M.

SOUVENIR

● PROGRAMME ●

Visits of foreign teams to Britain always arouse great interest. The Arsenal v. Sparta friendly of 1946 (note that this is a pirate issue) was no exception; remember that World War Two had only just finished.

The centre pages of the 1937/8 Birmingham v. Middlesbrough programme display a typical range of advertisements from that era.

BLACKPOOL

v.

PRESTON NORTH END

Saturday, December 13th, 1947

Kick-off 2.15 p.m.

OFFICIAL PROGRAMME 2ᴰ·

In 1947/8, both Blackpool and Preston were fighting for honours in Division One – the fortunes of both clubs have since changed dramatically.

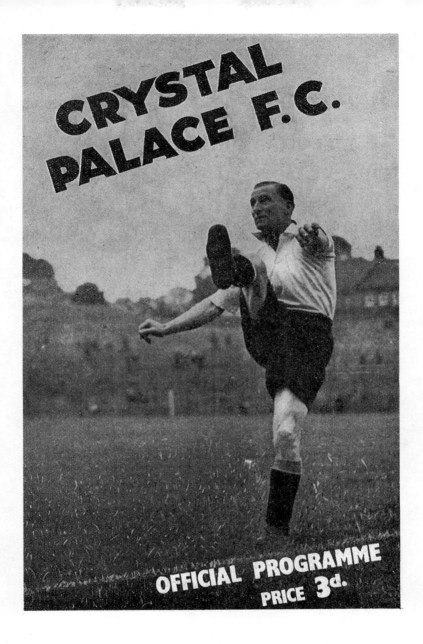

The cover of the 1946/7 Crystal Palace v. Swindon programme provides a fine study of the typical 1940's player, and highlights the total contrast in style with the modern player.

Hull City's 1956/7 programme uses the nickname of the club, 'The Tigers', to good effect in this striking cover design.

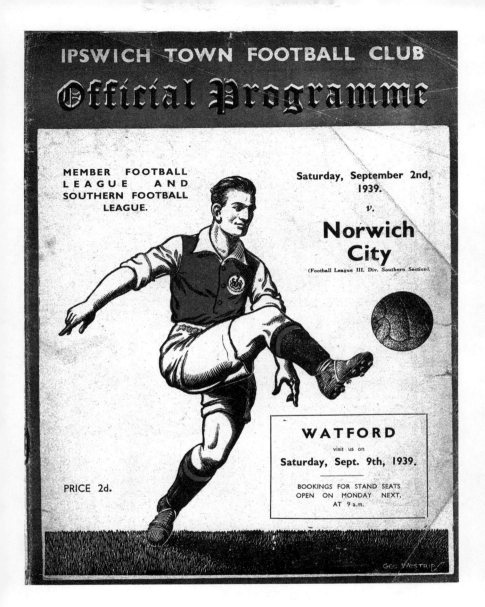

IPSWICH TOWN FOOTBALL CLUB
Official Programme

MEMBER FOOTBALL LEAGUE AND SOUTHERN FOOTBALL LEAGUE.

Saturday, September 2nd, 1939.

v.

Norwich City
(Football League III. Div. Southern Section).

WATFORD
visit us on
Saturday, Sept. 9th, 1939.

BOOKINGS FOR STAND SEATS OPEN ON MONDAY NEXT, AT 9 a.m.

PRICE 2d.

GEO WESTRIP

Ipswich Town met Norwich City in the 1939/40 Division Three South local 'derby', little realising that due to the devastation of World War Two, this was to be their last match for several years.

THE NOTTS COUNTY

3D

NOTTS COUNTY

Vol. XXXIV No. 14   VERSUS   December 25th, 1954

BRISTOL ROVERS

At first glance, there is nothing unusual about this 1954 Notts County programme. In modern football, however, how many teams play their matches on Christmas Day? Such fixtures were once commonplace.

The 1959/60 Southampton programme incorporates 'The Saints' club nickname into a simple, but attractive, design.

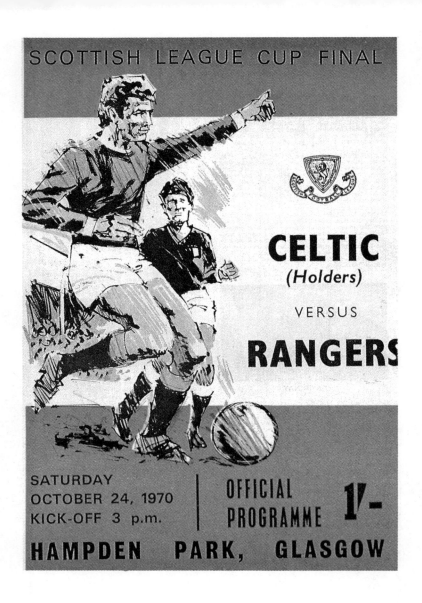

The 'Old Firm' meet again in the 1970 Scottish League Cup Final. On this occasion Rangers triumph 1–0.